ITALIAN JEWISH COOKING

MIRA SACERDOTI

HILL *of* CONTENT

MELBOURNE

First published in Australia by
Hill of Content Publishing 1992
86 Bourke Street, Melbourne 3000

Designed by Julian Jones

Illustrated by Mira Sacerdoti

Cover photograph by Ron Sacerdoti

Typeset by Midland Typesetters, Maryborough 3465
Printed by Australian Print Group, Maryborough 3465

National Library
Cataloguing-in-Publication data:

Sacerdoti, Mira, 1928–
    Italian Jewish cooking.

    Includes index.
    ISBN 0 85572 208 8.

    1. Cooking, Jewish. 2. Cooking, Italian.
    I. Erlich, Rita, II. Title.
641.56767

Contents

In memory of
Mama and Nonna Rina,
and for Riccardo,
Michael and Ron.

Editor's Foreword

Tell me what you eat; I will tell you what you are. (Brillat-Savarin, La Physiologie du Gout)

We reveal much about ourselves by what we eat, how we eat, when we eat and with whom. Mira Sacerdoti's book tells us about herself—about her childhood, her adolescence, her married life, her family, and her husband's family. It also tells us something about the richness of the Jewish communities in Italy.

Jewish cooking has only recently been receiving the wide attention it deserves. Everyone interested in food knows about French cooking, and Italian cooking, and Chinese cooking. These are all now clearly defined by geography, by history, by culture and by economics. They are all well documented, most especially in the cooking of the wealthy, who had the money and the leisure to develop feasting to an art form.

In recent years, there has been mushrooming interest in food and cookery. The spores were set earlier this century by a Frenchman who called himself Curnonsky and gave new dignity to regional French cooking by recognising its distinctive styles. It was a radical departure from earlier studies which had focussed on haute cuisine. Since then, and notably since the Second World War, food writers have been exploring different styles of cooking and eating with the same insatiable curiosity as explorers in centuries past headed off into worlds unknown.

We have been told about the cooking of all the countries of the West and the Orient, everything from the regional cuisines of France and Italy to the traditional foods of Wales and Ireland, of India, of Laos and Vietnam, Thailand and Japan, the Caribbean and the Pacific islands. Through books and magazine articles, we have been privy to the re-invention and re-interpretation of dishes by a host of young chefs.

There has been a veritable fireworks display of cooking. No country has been exempt, no region so remote that its cooking could not be investigated and recorded. We have more than recipes now; we have history and anthropology, travel and research, celebrations of new approaches to cooking and eating and wakes for the old and moribund ways.

But Jewish cooking has kept a low profile throughout this cookery boom. Jewish cooking? What is that? Very simply, it is food prepared by Jews in accordance with Jewish dietary laws. Jewish cooking keeps dairy foods and meat quite separate, and disallows certain meats and seafoods. The laws are ancient. They are given in the Bible and have been codified by centuries of written and oral tradition.

The laws are clear enough. But it is only recently that Jewish cooking has been the subject of the same interest as other cuisines of the world. There are good reasons for that. Other styles of cooking may be defined geographically and socially, but Jewish cooking is defined by religious law. To make it more difficult, there have been Jewish communities throughout the world for thousands of years. What might we mean by Jewish cooking? The cooking of the Jews of England, of India, of Egypt, of Syria, of Russia, of Poland?

Many of those communities have disappeared now. The cataclysmic anti-Semitism that lead to the deaths of millions of Jews before and during the Second World War meant the disappearance of whole communities. The Holocaust meant the end of a civilisation, as monumental as the fall of Troy, or of Constantinople. The enormity of the loss meant many things. It certainly left no one in a mood to record recipes.

Jewish cooking is pre-eminently family cooking. There may well have been a court tradition of cooking (in Spain and in Babylon), but throughout that period we know as modern history, Jewish cooking has been home-based. It has been food for the family, and for the extended family, food for sustenance and hospitality. It has been cooking for everyday, and cooking to celebrate the many festivals that are part of the Jewish calendar.

Like all family cooking, its traditions have been oral for the most part. Recipes have been passed from mother to daughter, and from mother-in-law to daughter-in-law. While the traditions of family life were alive and well, no one would have bothered to write them down (even assuming that women in all communities were educated enough to write). The first specifically Jewish cookbooks appeared about 160 years ago, first in the United States and then in England. Their appearance argues a new literacy, a new mobility, and even a kind of dislocation. Who needed a book when she had a mother or mother-in-law or aunts to teach her?

Many mothers and mothers-in-law and aunts were lost during the Second World War. Those who survived those years in Europe were often lucky enough just to eat. When they rebuilt their lives, and as food supplies returned to normal, they gradually rebuilt the patterns of daily eating. Jewish cooking, however, has been subject to the changes of all other kinds of cooking in developed countries over the last forty years or so. All cooking evolves in time, adapts to the changing availability of food supplies, to changing family size, to different work patterns, to new industries and technology.

The children of those who survived and escaped the war are now old enough to want to reach out for some of the evidence of their parents' early lives. Most of them have children of their own, which makes tangible a sense of continuity and, as adults and as parents, they see their parents in a new light. What were their early lives like? What were their own childhoods like? Food and cooking are small ways of knowing about the past and rediscovering it. That is why we are seeing a renewed interest in Jewish cooking. It is also true that the generation of the war years is now ageing; their children and grandchildren recognise the need to record family histories before they are lost for good. Family recipes are part of those histories.

This book grew out of a request from Mira Sacerdoti's children that she write down all the recipes they knew and loved. That is normal family life, a tribute to a mother's cooking skills. But the disappearance of Jewish communities in Italy gave her task a special poignance.

These recipes represent a personal history. They also show a little of the venerable history of the Jews in Italy. There have been Jews in Italy since Roman times, coming and going with the centuries. They came with the Romans, as slaves or as traders; they came as refugees from Spain before and after the Inquisition; they came from Central and Eastern Europe. Each group has its own name: Italkim (those from Italy), Sephardim (those from Spain—Sepharad being the old Hebrew name for Spain), and Ashkenazim (Ashkenaz being the old Hebrew name for Germany).

Each group has its own ways. Within Italy, which has always been markedly regionalised, there would have been regional variations. Within the regions, there would also have been variations from city to city and from village to village, even from family to family.

Those variations can be tracked in this book. Look at the different versions of dishes as cooked by Nonna Rina and Zia Tilde, look at the different regional versions of festive foods like Harosset, one of the ritual dishes of Passover.

There are certain combinations of flavours and ingredients that suggest ancient origins, such as the use of vinegar, oil, pine nuts and sultanas in a single dish. The sweet-sourness of that combination is typical of ancient Roman cooking (insofar as we can make judgments of it).

In my notes on many recipes, I have observed Sephardic influences. It is unlikely that all those recipes date from the 15th century; many of them must have come from other Sephardi communities around the Mediterranean. For example, the use of egg and lemon in sauces points to a Sephardi origin of those dishes, but who can now tell where the Sephardi origins began?

It is possible that those egg and lemon dishes came out of Greece. Egg and lemon sauce is characteristic of Greek cooking. We know that many Jews came to Thessaloniki in the 15th century as refugees from Inquisition persecutions in Spain, Sicily, southern Italy and Portugal and were settled there by Sultan Bayezid II. While Greece was part of the Ottoman empire, Jews played an important role in commerce for some time. People in trade and commerce travelled; they travelled and they picked up new ideas, they travelled and they married, and the women they married brought with them all their own family recipes and learnt new recipes from their mothers-in-law. Perhaps that is how egg and lemon dishes came to Italian-Jewish cooking. Who knows exactly how? Perhaps those trading families moved to Italy, perhaps members of the Italian families visited and liked what they ate so much they took recipes back to Italy, perhaps children were married to someone from their mother's home-town, perhaps...

Much of this must necessarily be speculation. We know quite a lot about the life of Jews in Italy and other Mediterranean countries, but we know almost nothing about what they ate in centuries past. Most historians do not have anything to say about cooking and eating.

But we get a different version of history from cookbooks, and from Mira Sacerdoti's book. It is personal, it is differently structured, but from the recipes we can glimpse moments of the way things were in times past and centuries gone.

The recipes in this book are for dishes to be enjoyed. Not all of them are equally appropriate for modern kitchens and tastes, but all of them have been made by Mira Sacerdoti, and most of them have been made by many women before her. These dishes are the taste of history and the pleasure of the present. They are dishes made out of respect for the ancient Jewish dietary laws, and with pride in cooking skills, and with love for the families, friends and guests for whom they were prepared.

This is unmistakably Italian food, and distinctively Jewish food. Some of these dishes, those called *alla Giudea* (in the Jewish style), have become part of the wider Italian repertoire, but many of them will be unfamiliar to readers. The range and diversity of vegetable dishes, always one of the strengths of Italian cooking, will appeal to modern tastes, although many of them show a way of life and cooking that has nearly disappeared. Some of them, like spinach roots and pea pods, are extravagant in their use of labour, and they show respect for the preciousness of produce.

This book is a tribute to precious things—to food, and ceremonial tables, and to the skills of generations of women. My thanks go to Mira Sacerdoti for allowing me to share the knowledge of them.

Rita Erlich 1992

Introduction

There are many Italian cookbooks on the market because Italian food is delicious and therefore very popular. But traditional Italian-Jewish cooking is not well known. Indeed the fact that one is an Italian and a Jew is often met with astonishment and the invariable question—'Are there Jews in Italy?' The second question is: 'Do they eat a lot of pasta?' The answer to both questions is yes.

Are there Jews in Italy? Of course there are, and there have been for a long time. Think of Shakespeare's 'Merchant of Venice', first of all. And then go back in time. Those who have been to Rome might have visited the Jewish Catacombs of Rome, or the catacombs of Villa Torlonia and Vigna Randanini with their familiar symbols of the menorah (branched candelabra) and other Jewish symbols.

There have been Jews in Italy for more than two thousand years, since long before Italy existed in its present political form. The first Jews settled in Rome during the second century BC, and they came to Rome then and thereafter as traders, as exiles, and as slaves. It is estimated that there were about 50,000 to 60,000 Jews in Rome when

1

Tiberius was emperor (14–37AD), and about forty other Jewish settlements in Italy. After the destruction of the Temple in Jerusalem by the Romans in the year 70, countless thousands of Jewish slaves were brought to Rome; Titus's arch in Rome still stands, nearly 2000 years after it was built, and still shows the Temple Menorah he captured carved on the stone.

Jews came and went throughout Italy. We forget how much people travelled in centuries past, for all the reasons they still journey—curiosity, trade and commerce, escape from oppression. Jews settled in Rome first of all—the Jewish community there is probably the oldest in the Diaspora—and over 2000 years they settled in all parts of Italy. They lived in various cities, and they came peacefully to those areas under Moslem control or influence. They settled in Sicily, for example, and there was a large and prosperous Jewish community there until they were expelled by a Spanish royal edict in 1492. That year, the year of the Inquisition, saw the expulsion of Jews from all Spanish territories, and many of the survivors found their way to those parts of Italy that were more or less hospitable to Jews.

There were Jews in many parts of Italy before that. There were Jews in Venice, no doubt from the time Venice established itself as a major trading centre in the tenth century. The Giudecca of Venice is so called because Jews were obliged to live there in the 13th century. We know they existed in the university towns of Turin, Mantua and Bologna. We know that Jews, expelled from medieval towns in England and Germany, often found refuge in Italy, where attitudes to Jews were fairly tolerant even in the later Middle Ages.

At present there are 30,000 Jews in Italy. The largest communities are in Rome, (15,000) and in Milan (9,500). The remaining 5,000 are scattered all over Italy.

Italian Jewish cooking evolved simultaneously with the development of regional Italian cooking. It evolved, too, with the successive waves of Jewish immigration over the centuries. Historical records are by and large silent on matters of food, but occasionally we find hints of what people ate. Fennel and eggplant, for example, were regarded as Jewish food, even into the 19th century—at least in Florence, where a cookbook published in 1890 noted that even forty years earlier, those two vegetables were scarcely seen on the Florentine market because they were regarded as foods of the Jews.

Successive waves of Jewish immigration must have influenced Jewish diet in Italy: the Italkim (Jews from Italy) would have eaten slightly differently from the Sephardim (Jews from Spain) and the Ashkenazim (Jews from Central and Eastern Europe).

We can make some guesses about who ate what. The prevalence of sweet and sour flavours in many fish dishes, known as *alla Ebraica* or *alla Giudea* (in the Hebrew or Jewish style) seems very like the ingredients and flavours of ancient Roman cookery. We can only speculate that there might be a cooking tradition that goes back 2000 years. But the similarities between certain Italian-Jewish dishes and those from Sephardic communities in the Middle East suggests they both had common origin in the Jewish communities who lived in Spain for centuries until they were finally expelled during the Inquisition. (In Hebrew Sepharad is the old word for Spain, Sephardim are those from Spain.)

In time, their different eating habits would have adapted to the regions in which they lived over generations. Their diets would have been like Jewish cooking all over the world in following the Jewish dietary laws; that is, their food was kosher. Orthodox Jewish housewives are well versed in the laws of kosher cooking and the keeping of a kosher kitchen, therefore I will not presume to explain kashrut at any length but will indicate, for general interest, the basic rules of a kosher kitchen.

Kosher cooking is based on dietary laws established on common sense and hygiene in biblical times. The laws of kosher cooking are the same everywhere, irrespective of the cook's country of birth or residence. The great variety of kosher cooking that we enjoy today evolved over the ages with the migration of Jewish communities from country to country and from continent to continent. Local ingredients were used and variations of basic recipes became the local kosher dishes as we know them today. The variety of ingredients used in kosher cooking is limited only by the dietary laws of kashrut.

Kashrut means that:
All vegetables and cereals may be eaten, but only if meticulously cleaned and washed.

Fish may only be eaten if, in its natural state, it has both fins and scales. All other fish and shellfish are forbidden.

Eggs must be broken separately into a glass dish and examined for traces of blood. If blood or any sign of fertilisation is present, the egg must be discarded. Eggs found in poultry when the poultry is slaughtered may be used only with meat dishes.

Poultry and animals that chew the cud and have cloven feet may be eaten. Game, game birds, pigs and all products of the same are forbidden. No blood may be present in kosher meat, poultry or any products thereof. To be kosher, animals, as well as poultry, must be slaughtered in a specific way under rabbinical supervision.

All milk and dairy products may be eaten. Milk and meat may not be cooked or served in the same utensils, nor may they be eaten together. Milk and meat dishes must not be placed in the oven (or dishwasher), at the same time. After meat is eaten several hours must elapse before dairy food of any kind may be eaten.

All manufactured foods must be sealed and must bear the rabbinical stamp. The stamp certifies that the food was manufactured and packaged under rabbinical supervision according to the law of kashrut. The same rules apply to all washing up and cleaning materials used in the kosher kitchen.

In a kosher kitchen different and easily recognisable cooking utensils, china, cutlery, washing bowls, sink bowls, working surfaces, dishwashers and fridges must be used for the preparation and storage of milk and meat dishes. Different kitchen and table linen is used for the cleaning and serving of kosher food. All utensils used for the preparation, serving and cleaning of dishes with milk or dairy food must be kept in separate cupboards from those used for meat dishes. Traditionally the utensils and linen used for milk dishes had a blue pattern while those used for meat dishes have a red pattern, whilst either can be used for fish.

For Pesach the kitchen is cleaned so thoroughly and meticulously that not a crumb of any food remains anywhere. All the kitchen and serving utensils are cleaned according to ritual and only food that is Kosher le Pesach can be used. In most kosher households a complete separate set of cooking and serving utensils, as well as kitchen and table linen, are kept only for use during the Pesach week. The kitchen is ready for Pesach when the housewife has gathered and burned the last crumbs of bread and has recited the appropriate blessing (see Pesach, under 'Holidays and Menus for Holidays').

The Sabbath

The Sabbath is considered the queen of the week, a day of rest that is often regarded as the most important holiday of the Jewish year, and yields its importance only to the Day of Atonement.

Symbolically, the Sabbath represents the bride as well as the seventh day of the creation of the world, the day of rest.

The Sabbath, as all other Holidays, begins at sunset. To ensure that resting during the Sabbath is complete no manual labour is to be undertaken and, as no fire may be lit, no cooking may be done. The food for the Sabbath is cooked on Friday afternoon and must be ready before sunset. The Sabbath meal is rich and festive. Traditionally it includes a first course, two main courses, one of fish and another of meat, a sweet, fruit and coffee.

By sunset on Friday, the home has a festive air. The table, according to tradition, is laid with a snow white tablecloth and the best dishes and cutlery. The Sabbath lights are placed on the table and the candles are lit by the mother of the family when the first star appears in the sky.

The meat is presided over by the father of the family. Very few of my generation have been fortunate enough to see our grandfathers at the Sabbath table.

SABBATH MENU
Tagliolini with Bagna Brusca
or
Sabbath Rice
Marinated Sole
or
Nonna Lea's Fish
Sabbath Veal
Veal
or
Poultry
Almond Torte
Coffee

Rosh Hashana
(New Year)

The Jewish calendar is calculated according to the phases of the moon. There are twelve months in the Jewish year, and thirteen in the leap year, which comes more frequently than the quadrennial leap year of the international calendar. That means that all Jewish holidays fall each year on a different date of the modern calendar. The counting of the years is reckoned differently, too, beginning (according to one tradition) with the creation of the world or (according to another tradition), with Abraham. Thus A.D. 1990 was the 5751 of the Jewish calendar.

According to biblical tradition, the months are counted from Nissan, in the spring, but the new year, Rosh Hashana, is celebrated on the first day of Tishre, which is at the beginning of the northern hemisphere autumn.

Rosh Hashana also initiates the beginning of the ten days of penitence which culminate on the tenth day of Tishre with the celebration of Yom Kippur, the Day of Atonement.

In Italy the first meal of Rosh Hashana begins with apple slices dipped in honey, in the hope of a fruitful and sweet New Year. That custom also exists in many other Jewish communities, although a piece of halla often substitutes for the apple, and sugar is used instead of honey.

The celebration of Rosh Hashana, as of all Jewish holidays, begins and ends at sunset.

ROSH HASHANA MENU

Stroncatelli
or
Ricciolini
or
Calzoncini
Red Mullet alla Mosaica
Turkey Loaf
Baked or Fried Pumpkin
Vegetables in Season (without vinegar)
Apple Cake
or
Sfratti
or
Apples and Bananas with Rum

Yom Kippur
Day of Atonement

Yom Kippur is the most solemn of the holidays.

It is the concluding day of the ten days of penitence, and is a day of fasting and prayer. The fast begins at sunset on the ninth day of the month of Tishre and concludes at sunset of the next day, the tenth of Tishre, with the blowing of the Shofar (Ram's Horn).

During the fast no food or drink is allowed to pass the lips, so the meal served on the eve of Yom Kippur, although abundant, is free of spices.

The fast is broken with a repast of Focaccia (cake) with tea or coffee, followed later with a meal.

YOM KIPPUR MENU
Breaking the Fast
Tagliolini or Ricciolini in Soup
Triglie with Sultanas and Pine Nuts
Boiled Turkey
or
Turkey Loaf
Pizette with Marsala
or
Pizette of Heart
Dictinobis and Zabaione
Bruscatella di Kippur
Tea or Coffee

Succot
Feast of the Harvest

Succot is celebrated over a whole week, from the eve of the fifteenth to the sunset of the forteenth of Tishre (October), the time of the harvest in the northern hemisphere. Succot concludes with Simchat Torah, the celebration of the Torah.

In any available open space of the home, such as a balcony, terrace or garden, a Succah (hut) is constructed using only fronds, branches and twigs. The Succah is decorated with all the seasonal fruits and vegetables to represent the bounty of the Harvest.

During the seven days of Succot all meals are served in the Succah and as much time as possible is spent receiving visitors in the Succah.

During Succot a lot of stuffed food is prepared and cakes are made with fruit. In an Italian Succah the Bollo is never missing.

SUCCOT MENU
Minestrone Vegetable Soup
or
Pasticcio of Beets
Ginetti
or
Tagliatelle Cake
Bollo-o-Bollo

Simchat Torah
Rejoicing of the Law

Simchat Torah is celebrated on the twenty-third day of Tishre (October). At every Service in the Synagogue an established portion (Parashah) of the Torah is read, so that every year the entire Torah, the Five Books of Moses, are read. On Simchat Torah, the reading of the last portion of the yearly cycle of the Torah, as well as that of the first portion of the next cycle, is joyously celebrated.

The five scrolls of the Torah are carried through the Synagogue. Children participate in the celebration, joining the adults in song and in the blessing of the scrolls when touching them as they are carried past.

On Simchat Torah, the last day of Succot, vine leaves stuffed with meat and rice are usually served to remind us of the vineyards of Judea. If vine leaves are not available, cabbage leaves are used as a substitute.

SIMCHAT TORAH MENU
Stuffed Vine Leaves

Hanuckah

Hanuckah is celebrated over the period of eight days, from the eve
of the twenty-fifth of Kislef (December).

Hanuckah commemorates the heroic victory of the Maccabees over
Antiochus of Syria in 165 BC and celebrates the miracle of the oil. When,
after the devastation of the battle, the Maccabees cleansed the Temple
for re-dedication, they found enough sacred oil to light the menorah
(lamp), for one day only—then a miracle occurred and the oil burnt
for eight days.

The holiday begins with the lighting of the first light in the Hanuckya,
the nine-armed Hanuckah lamp. The family gathers around the Hanuckya
and, whilst the whole family sings the Hanuckah song, the youngest
child lights the first candle or tiny oil lamp. Each evening the ceremony
is repeated and one more candle is lit, until the last evening when eight
candles are alight. The ninth candle, the Shamash (Helper), is used only
to light the other candles.

Fried sweets are served during Hanuckah. The use of oil (instead
of candles) is not confined to the lighting of the lamps. During the
week of Hanuckah serving foods fried in oil is traditional in all Jewish
communities throughout the world.

HANUCKAH MENU
Spinach Ravioli
or
Rice with Sultanas
Impannate
Fried Hanuckah Chicken
or
Meat alla Shimshon
Eggplant alla Giudea
Precipizi

Sabbath Beshalach
The Miracle of the Red Sea

On this Sabbath we read the Parasha (a chapter of the Torah) that speaks of the miracle of the passage through the Red Sea.

When Moses led the Jews in their flight from Egypt, the Red Sea opened to allow them to cross and closed again behind them to drown the soldiers of the pursuing Pharaoh's Army. To the best of my knowledge the rather macabre tradition of marking this particular Sabbath with a special noodle cake is kept only in Italy.

The cake is called Ruota di Faraone (Pharaoh's Wheel). The cake is baked in the form of a wheel, the noodles remind us of the waves of the sea, the little pieces of goose salami and the sultanas remind us of the heads of the Egyptians floating in the sea...

In Venice, the cake is known as Frisenal, and it is called Hamin in Ferrara.

Only in Italy is Shabbath Beshalach celebrated as a festival. The chapter is known and read everywhere, but nowhere else is the day a day of celebration.

Tu B'Shvat
New Year of the Trees

Tu B'Shvat is celebrated on the fifteenth of Shvat (February), when the trees in the northern hemisphere begin to sprout new leaves.

Children plant new trees, and receive in return baskets of fresh and dried fruit. Schools and the children's rooms in the home are decorated with branches of blossoming fruit trees.

TU B'SHVAT MENU
Tortellini
or
Liver Pâté
Marinated Sole
Chicken and Rice
or
Beans
Sweet and Sour Cabbage
Cake with Apples

Purim

Purim is on the fourteenth of Adar (March).

Purim begins with the reading of the Megilah (Story) of Queen Ester and her Uncle Mordechai who foiled the plot of Haman, the minister of the Persian king Ahasuerus, to exterminate all the Jews of the Persian empire.

As it commemorates one of the very rare happenings in the Jewish history, a tragic event that ended in happiness, Purim is celebrated with gaiety.

Purim is a feast for young and old. Visits and presents are exchanged, masquerades are held, recitals are given by children in costume, wine and all sorts of sweets are eaten in abundance. It is the one time of the Jewish year when drunkenness is not abhorred, and it sometimes seems that the licences of Purim correspond to the permitted excesses of the Mardi Gras that precedes Lent in the Christian calendar.

Purim is a time of celebration, but it is also a time for giving charity, and a time to send gifts of food (cakes and fruit) to family and friends. It has been suggested that the gifts of cakes are one way of using up flour, since Purim is the last festival before Pesach, when no flour may remain in the house. There are all kinds of traditional cakes, but the Italian constant is a confection known as Orecchie di Haman (Haman's Ears), although who can guess why the ears of a villain should be a particular delicacy? In Italy Purim cakes are traditionally made with almonds.

PURIM MENU
Spinach Ravioli
Turkey Loaf
or
Pickled Veal and Beef
Fried Spinach
Buricche

Pesach
Exodus from Egypt

Pesach begins on the eve of the fifteenth of Nissan (late March or early April), and lasts seven days.

Pesach celebrates the Exodus of the Jews from Egypt. The Exodus is commemorated with the Seder, the ceremonial dinner, on the eve of the first day of Pesach in Israel and on the eve of the first two days of Pesach in the Diaspora.

During the Seder dinner the Hagadah is read. The Hagadah—the word means narration—was originally part of the general prayer book, but was copied separately from the 11th and 12th century. Hagadot were among the chief objects of ritual art, and many finely illuminated manuscripts have survived. One of them, known as the Sarajevo Hagadah because it is now in the Sarajevo Jewish Museum, is thought to date from the 13th century in Spain; we know that it was brought from Italy because of a handwritten comment... There were also some fine printed illustrated editions, including those printed in Mantua in 1560 and Venice in 1629.

In 1944 in Bari, during the allied occupation, the 179 Transport Company (Plugah Ivrit L'ovala), of the Jewish Brigade organised a communal Seder for Jewish refugees. In a classroom of an abandoned school, long trestle tables were set with army issue metal plates and cutlery, and on each plate lay a Hagadah. The Hagadot were handwritten and illustrated, printed, cut and stapled by the soldiers and officers of the 179. I still have and treasure mine.

For Pesach the home is thoroughly spring-cleaned and the kitchen is cleaned so meticulously that not a crumb of food is left anywhere. All the kitchen and serving utensils are cleansed according to ritual. Only food that is Kosher le Pesach can be used. In most kosher households a complete set of cooking and serving utensils is kept solely for use ·during the week of Pesach. The kitchen is ready for Pesach when the housewife has gathered and burned the last crumbs of bread and has recited the appropriate blessing.

During the week of Pesach no leavened food may be eaten. Matzot (azzime in Italian), the unleavened, unsalted bread, is eaten instead of any other bread. Many dishes and cakes are cooked with eggs, almonds and matza-meal, (coarsely or finely ground matzot). In some Italian communities corn-flour is used but, to prevent any possibility of fermentation, the corn-flour must be blended with eggs only, without water, and the mixture must be baked as soon as the corn-flour and eggs are mixed together.

In Hebrew Seder means order. The Seder Dinner is so called because it follows a specific order.

Around the Seder Dinner table family and friends are assembled for the reading of the Hagadah, the story of the Exodus. All the family participate in the telling of the story, particularly the children, who ask questions and make comments. The reading of the Hagadah is followed by the traditional meal.

For the Seder the table is covered with a fine white cloth and, in addition to the festive table setting, there must also be on the table:

1. a special threefold napkin to hold three matzot, one between each fold, to remind us of unleavened bread;

2. a wine glass for the Prophet Elija;

3. the Seder Salver on which are laid the ingredients used during the reading of the Hagadah;

4. a Hagadah (the book that narrates the story of the Exodus), for each participant;

5. enough wine for at least four glasses for each adult and four sips for each child;

6. hard-boiled eggs served in saltwater or vinegar to begin the dinner;

7. finger bowls.

In many Italian families the Seder table cloth and napkins and the trifold matzot napkin are elaborately hand embroidered and are, together with the ornate silver Seder Salver, passed down the generations from mother to first-born daughter or the wife of the first-born son.

The Seder Salver is placed next to the head of the family, who conducts the Seder ceremony. On the Seder Salver are the ingredients which remind us of the time when our ancestors were slaves in Egypt:

1. a burned lamb bone reminds us of the sacrificial lamb;

2. a hard-boiled egg singed on an open flame and immersed in salted water reminds us of the bitterness of slave labour;

3. harosset—a mixture of walnuts, grated apples and honey—reminds us of the heavy mortar and stones carried by slaves;

4. carpas—a lettuce leaf, a sprig of parsley and other greens—dipped in salt water reminds us of the tears shed in bondage;

5. marror—horse radish and bitter herbs—remind us how bitter the loss of freedom is.

Pesach Menu

FIRST SEDER DINNER
Hard-boiled Eggs in Salt Water
Sfoglietti in Chicken Soup with Fresh Peas
or
Broken Matzot in Chicken Soup
Red Mullet alla Mosaica
Turkey Loaf
Artichokes and Spinach
Scodellini con Amaretti
or
Zuccherini

SECOND SEDER DINNER
Hard-boiled Eggs in Salt Water
Dayenu
or
Scacchi
Boiled Chicken and Goose Breasts
or
Pickled Tongue
Peas and Artichokes

Shavuot

Shavuot, which means 'weeks' in Hebrew, falls seven weeks after Pesach, on the sixth of Sivan (June).

On Shavuot thanks are given for the Laws received on Mount Sinai.

Shavuot is also the feast of the first fruit. It was on this day that pilgrimage was made to the Synagogue with the offerings of the first fruit of the year.

On Shavuot the Synagogue is decorated with flowers, particularly roses. In recent years in Italy a new tradition evolved—girls celebrate their Bat Mizvah on Shavuot.

In some Italian communities no meat is eaten or wine drunk on Shavuot. Milk is one of the symbols of spring, and only meals based on milk are prepared. Dairy products are traditional in other communities as well.

SHAVUOT MENU
Gnocchi alla Romana
or
Baked Spinach with Ricotta
Torta di Shavuot
or
Jewish Pizza
Fennel
Galette for Shavuot
Torta di Cioccolato
Mount Sinai with Eggs

The Importance of Flour

To give due importance to flour I want to tell you about flour and bread during the war years we spent as refugees in Vela Luka, on the island of Korcula.

About once a month we were issued a carefully weighed quantity of so-called flour. How much flour we received varied according to the amount of flour that arrived from the mainland, as well as to the number of adults and children there were in the family.

What the flour was made of was anybody's guess, suffice it to say that it was of a dismal dirt-brown colour and that the resulting bread could have been put to good use in the building trade. But, of course, to us it was very precious.

Each time Uncle brought the flour home there was a ceremony. The family gathered around Uncle while he meticulously weighed the correct amount of flour to be sent to the baker in exchange for a few day's supply of bread.

My cousin Vera and I took turns to take the flour to the baker. The baker, holding up the ancient scales, made a ritual of weighing the flour again, then carefully writing the quantity into his ledger. Only then did he weigh the bread and hand it over with a big grin. It was always a small loaf plus a small piece extra to make up the correct weight. I often wondered why it was that only when I went to the baker did we get that extra bit. Vera still denies eating it on the way home from the baker.

Uncle solemnly sliced the bread, carefully measuring each slice. Mama, Aunty, Vera and I received one thin slice a day while Uncle, because he was a man, allowed himself two thicker slices. I loved Uncle dearly but he certainly never heard of 'women and children first'.

One day one of the trawlers that, quite unexpectedly, sometimes brought some food to the island (see recipe for chips), Uncle brought home a small parcel of grey powder. Nobody knew what it was. Uncle said it must be cement. Aunty dramatically stated she would not have a bar of it—it could only be ground glass, she said. Flabbergasted, Vera and I looked at our elders, awaiting each new verdict with bated breath. Then Mama smelled it, put it on the kitchen table, poked it with her finger and gingerly tasted it. With a look of stunned disbelief she burst into laughter: 'It is flour!'

The five of us stood around the table and debated what delicacy Mama could concoct with this unexpected bonanza. As it befitted her, Mama had the last word on culinary matters and her decision was to make pancakes.

We had not seen either an egg or milk since before the war, but that was no problem for my Mama. Mama explained that she would make the pancakes with the flour and water. We could then fill the precious pancakes with a slice of the concrete block of goo that we were given months ago under the name of jam.

It is anybody's guess what the so-called jam was made of. It looked like solidified shoe polish and smelled not much better. It was dark brown and very sticky, with a texture unlike anything edible that I had ever tasted before. But I was only thirteen years old and, as I was frequently told, I had a lot to learn. Anyway when the goo was mashed and diluted with a little water it still looked ghastly but it definitely tasted sweetish.

Once the decision to make pancakes was unanimously approved, I was sent to Donna Maria to fetch water. Donna Maria lived on top of the village hill from where she gloated at the whole population of our village. She had the only well in the village, with water that always tasted fresh and never dried out. In summer, Donna Maria's well often became our only source of drinking water. I promised Donna Maria a pancake and she allowed me to draw a pail of water.

It was not yet lunch time but that was irrelevant because we were always hungry, particularly Vera and I. We never starved—we just never had enough food.

As soon as I brought the water Mama started to mix her pancakes. Uncle, Aunty, Vera and I stood around the stove and carefully watched Mama's every move. Mama put the flour into a bowl and added the water very slowly. When she was satisfied with the consistency of the batter she added a pinch of salt. Now Mama was ready, she heated a teaspoon of our virgin olive oil in a frying pan, and when the oil was hot she poured a little bit of the mixture into the hot, green oil, twisting the pan every which way to spread the batter. We held our breath as the batter in the heavy iron frying pan grew thinner and thinner, and larger and larger. And when the first pancake was ready there was a round of loud applause from Mama's rapt audience.

Before the applause ended we heard a very different noise—a noise we had all heard before and had no hesitation identifying. It was a German plane. We crowded in the door to have a look—the plane was flying so low that we saw the pilot looking down at us.

He circled over the village once then flew out to sea and discharged a burst of machine-gin fire into the waves, banked, turned, and kept coming closer and closer still shooting at full blast. The whole village was in a panic; everybody was running up the hill towards the vineyards; that is—everybody but my Mama.

Aunty, Uncle and Vera fled with everybody else. Over the din of the shooting plane a few villagers could still be heard shouting and running while I stood there, mesmerised—watching as Mama imperturbably continued to make pancakes.

The plane circled the village once more without hitting anybody. When, after the plane had disappeared in the distance, Aunty, Uncle and Vera returned, the kitchen table was set and two pancakes were sitting on each plate.

When the same plane—we knew its number and indeed recognised the pilot—returned every morning for several days, it was decided that everybody would leave the village and settle in the vineyards under the olive trees. The families who lodged with those villagers who had a vineyard were invited to share the watchman's hut. The huts were used in the middle of summer until the end of the harvest. When the grapes began to ripen a member of the owner's family, with a goat or two and his dogs, kept watch over the vineyard until the harvest was finished.

First Courses

Dough for Pasta and Soup Noodles

Jewish communities in Italy have adopted the local custom of serving pasta or rice as a first course instead of soup. You will find that the recipes for first courses give large quantities, because they are calculated to fill a generously heaped continental soup bowl.

Nonna Rina, my mother-in-law and first mentor in traditional Jewish cooking in Italy, calculated one chicken egg per adult and one pullet egg per child, with as much flour as it takes to obtain the right consistency of the dough, and I still follow her instructions. As our eggs are sold graded according to size it is easy to follow this rule. Commercial pasta is calculated at 100 g per adult and 50 g per child. However, these quantities can be adjusted according to your needs.

The pasta dough in this recipe is the basic dough used for most home-made pasta dishes such as tagliatelle, lasagna, tortellini, ravioli, Frisenal and many others.

INGREDIENTS:

    1 egg, lightly beaten
150 *g plain flour*
    1 dessertspoon water
      pinch of salt

Place the flour on the working surface, make a depression in the middle of the mound of flour then put all the remaining ingredients into the hollow.

Knead the dough until it forms a firm, smooth, round ball. Wrap the dough in a kitchen towel and let it rest, at room temperature, for about half an hour.

An easy alternative is to put all the ingredients into the Kenwood and work with the dough hook until the dough is smooth and remains attached to the hook. At that point turn the dough out onto the working bench and continue to work with the rolling pin.

Sprinkle the working surface lightly with plain flour, place the dough in the middle of the working bench and flatten it with a rolling pin. Work with the rolling pin rotating the dough until you obtain a thin, even sheet.

Sprinkle with a little flour and allow the dough to rest for another 5 minutes.

Roll the whole sheet of dough up upon itself, and cut it (as you would slice a salami) about 5mm wide for noodles or as thin as you like them for soup noodles.

Noodles with 'Bagna Brusca' or 'Agresto'
For Bagna Brusca and Agresto (see Sauces)

Nonna Rina called this dish the 'lazy girl's pasta' for some reason. You cannot afford to be too lazy if it is to be good, because it is a simple and delicious dish when made with fresh pasta and the pan juices of roasted chickens.

INGREDIENTS:

> 800 g thinly sliced egg noodles
>   juices from a roast
>   or
>   olive oil
>   freshly ground pepper
>   salt

Boil the noodles in abundant water. When the noodles are al dente, drain and toss the noodles to rid them of all the water. Put the noodles on a cold surface or into a large shallow dish, and pour the gravy or olive oil over them.

With a fork in each hand, gently take the noodles from the bottom of the dish and pull them through the sauce. Repeat this operation until the noodles are cold and have absorbed most of the sauce.

Put onto a chilled serving dish and serve with Salsa Brusca or tomato sauce. See page 212 for Salsa Brusca.

Cold Noodles

This is an easy dish to make for lunch because it can be made in advance and kept in the refrigerator for several hours.

INGREDIENTS:

> 600 g plain flour
>   6 eggs
>   1 dessertspoon water or stock
>   1 kg peeled tomatoes
>   or
>   3 tablespoons tomato paste, diluted
>   1 cup olive oil
>   2 cloves of garlic, crushed
>   2 tablespoons chopped parsley
>   salt
>   half a hot chilli
>   or
>   freshly ground pepper

With the eggs, flour and water make the dough for noodles (see recipe), cut the noodles very thinly, spread them on a floured tray, cover with a tea towel and set aside.

Prepare a saucepan with ample salted water to boil the noodles.

In another saucepan heat the oil, garlic and hot chilli. Remove the garlic as soon as it is lightly coloured and add either the fresh peeled tomatoes or the diluted tomato paste, season with salt, pepper or chilli and boil briskly, uncovered. The sauce should not boil very long, 10–15 minutes should be sufficient to reduce it to the desired consistency.

Boil the noodles for 1–2 minutes, until al dente, drain and put the noodles into a preheated serving dish.

Mix the parsley into the sauce and pour the sauce over the noodles then, with a fork in each hand, gently take the noodles from the bottom of the dish and pull them through the sauce. Repeat this operation until the noodles are cold and have absorbed most of the sauce.

Serve chilled.

Serves 6

Ricciolini

This is an old recipe for soup pasta. Ricciolini were traditionally served at dinner on the eve of Yom Kippur. It is a recipe that comes from Ferrara but is widely used in other parts of Italy.

Prepare the dough for soup noodles (see recipe on page 20), but use more flour so that the dough is firmer. Knead until smooth, cover and set aside. Allow to rest for an hour.

Divide the dough into 4 parts. Take a piece of dough and roll it out with the rolling pin, until you have an even sheet of pastry about 5 mm thick.

Brush the pastry with oil and cut it into squares about 3 to 4 cm wide.

Hold a square of dough with your left hand and run your right thumb along its middle, pressing down firmly and evenly, so that you stretch the dough and at the same time curl it.

Spread the curls (riccioli) over a flat surface and sprinkle lightly with flour so that they do not stick.

Repeat this operation until all the pastry is curled, then bring the chicken soup to the boil, drop in all the pastry and boil until al dente.

Cannelloni

Traditionally cannelloni are made with the same dough as any other egg dough for pasta but with a little more flour to make it firmer than usual. Roll the pastry to the same thickness used for noodles then cut into 50 mm × 50 mm squares.

Boil the squares, a few at a time, in an abundant quantity of boiling salted water to which you have added a couple of tablespoons of olive oil. The water must be boiling briskly before the pasta squares are added, and they must be added carefully to avoid tearing them.

To avoid tearing the pasta when the squares are being filled you should:

drain the pasta before it is quite cooked;

arrange each drained square on a damp tea towel until it is all ready.

Put the filling of your choice along one side of each pasta square, roll it up and place it, fold down, in the bottom of an oiled baking dish. Arrange the cannelloni side by side and cover them with a thick tomato sauce.

Bake in a pre-heated oven at 350°F or 180°C for about 20 minutes, or until heated through.

The same fillings can be used for cannelloni as for pasticci.

Of course, cannelloni can be prepared with ready-made pasta. They should be boiled in the same way as the freshly-made squares—a few at a time in a lot of salted water to which some oil has been added.

Drain them as they are ready and arrange them on a damp tea towel until all the tubes are cooked.

Fill them with your preferred filling, using a teaspoon, and bake them as above.

Sabbat Beshalach Noodles

This dish is called Frisenal or Pharaoh's Wheel in Venice and Hamin in Ferrara. It is a dish traditionally served on Sabbat Beshalach, a holiday that seems to be celebrated only by the Jews in Italy.

INGREDIENTS:

> 400 g plain flour
>   4 eggs
> 100 g sultanas
> 100 g pine nuts
> 100 g goose salami
>   4 tablespoons roast beef gravy
>   or
>   2 tablespoons goose fat

Prepare the pastry for the noodles with the eggs and flour only, without adding water.

When the pastry is smooth and firm, roll it with the rolling pin until it is thin and even then, cut it into 3–4 mm wide noodles.

Plunge the noodles into a large saucepan of boiling, salted water and continue to boil until al dente. Drain and put the noodles into the dish with the gravy or goose fat, and, lifting the noodles with two forks, mix until the gravy is well distributed.

In a mixing bowl combine the chopped salami with the sultanas and pine nuts.

Preheat the oven to 350°F or 180°C.

In a round, oiled baking dish layer the noodles, alternating with the dry ingredients, beginning and ending with noodles, and bake until crisp and brown.

For a change, instead of baking the noodles, heat a little oil in a wide frying pan and stir fry the noodles until crisp.

Whichever way you prepare this dish, serve it as soon as it is ready.

Serves 6

Spezzatini

Spezzato means broken. Pasta called spezzatini or maltaglati are long hollow maccheroni broken by hand into pieces about 4 to 5 cm long. Because the pasta is broken by hand the pieces are uneven, hence the names of either 'spezzatini' i.e. broken ones, or 'maltagliati' i.e. badly cut ones.

Admittedly many pasta shapes prepared with a good sauce taste exactly the same, but I have had numerous complaints from my in-laws about serving the wrong shape of pasta with particular sauces.

INGREDIENTS:

> *500 g spezzatini, ziti*
> *or*
> *any other short pasta*
> *500 g chopped peeled tomatoes*
> *3 tablespoons olive oil*
> *1 tablespoon chopped parsley*
> *1 clove crushed garlic*
> *1 small chopped onion*
> *freshly ground pepper*
> *salt*

In a saucepan heat the oil, add the onion and the garlic, and discard the garlic as soon as it is lightly coloured. Add the tomatoes and salt and, stirring once or twice, continue to simmer for about 20 minutes.

Add the pasta and a little hot water then, stirring frequently, simmer until the pasta is al dente, adding more hot water if needed. When nearly ready, add the parsley and pepper.

The result should be a soup-like dish, served with grated Parmesan cheese.

Serves 6

Maccheroni Frittata

The staunch standby of every Italian cook—'frittata di maccheroni'—can be made with a mixture of freshly cooked pasta and sauce that has been prepared several hours in advance (if you mix fresh eggs into a freshly made pasta and sauce the result will be very tasty scrambled eggs), or, with any left-over pasta that may be at hand.

There are only two rigid rules in making a successful frittata: a. the pasta must not be very moist, hence the preference for left-over pasta that has had the time to absorb all the moisture even from a thin sauce, and b. the shape of the pasta. If the pasta used is not in the shape of the many long, thin varieties, or of the small, short varieties—cut it! This is not as difficult as it sounds, put the cooked, cold pasta into a glass bowl and, using a fork and a sharp knife, cut across the pasta, mix it and cut again turning the bowl every time you cut, until the pasta is not longer than 15–20 mm.

Frittata di maccheroni can be served hot or cold. It is a very tasty and practical dish for picnics and barbecues as it can be prepared in advance.

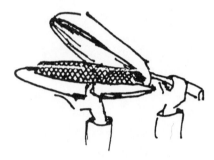

INGREDIENTS:

> *300 g pasta*
> *tomato or any other sauce of your choice*
> *Parmesan cheese*
> *4 large eggs*
> *olive oil*
> *freshly ground pepper*
> *salt*

Boil the pasta in a saucepan full of salted water, until al dente. Drain and transfer the pasta into a mixing bowl, add the sauce and mix well. Set aside for several hours, preferably overnight.

Add the Parmesan, pepper and eggs and mix with a fork until all the pasta is well coated with the eggs.

Heat a little oil in a wide frying pan. When the oil is hot remove excess, leaving only enough oil to coat the bottom and the sides of the frying pan.

Put the mixture into the hot, oiled frying pan, level the top with a spatula, lower the flame and place the frying pan so that the border of the frying pan sits on the flame. Move the frying pan clockwise, every few minutes, so that the frittata browns equally all over the base and sides. If the frying pan is left in the middle of the flame, the middle of the frittata will burn and the sides will remain uncooked.

When the base is browned and the frittata moves freely when you shake the pan, cover the frying pan with an inverted plate that is slightly larger than the frying pan. Holding, with both hands, plate and frying pan firmly together, turn upside down.

Slide the frittata back into the frying pan and continue to cook until brown on both sides. As the shape of frittata depends on the size of the frying pan, if the frittata is very thick, cook it very slowly to ensure that it is cooked through.

Serves 4-6

Pumpkin Tortellini

This recipe, very popular in Ancona and Ferrara, is prepared with variations according to the mood of the cook. The original recipe, I was told, is made with nutmeg but that is often replaced either by various other spices or even by finely chopped fried onion. However, I found that using fried onion causes the tortellini to open when immersed in boiling water. The tortellini can be served as a vegetable or as a first course.

INGREDIENTS:

> 500 *g pumpkin*
> 500 *g plain flour*
> 100 *g butter*
>   50 *g sultanas*
>   7 *tablespoons grated Parmesan cheese*
>   ½ *teaspoon grated nutmeg*
>   5 *eggs*
>   *bread crumbs*
>   *freshly ground pepper*
>   *salt*

With the flour and 4 of the eggs make the dough for pasta (see recipe page 20). At the same time bake the pumpkin until tender. Remove the skin and purée the pumpkin in the food processor or pass it through a sieve.

Combine the pumpkin purée with the remaining egg, the sultanas, three tablespoons of Parmesan cheese, a pinch of salt, pepper and nutmeg and blend well. If the mixture is very soft add enough bread crumbs to form a thick paste.

Roll out the dough into a thin sheet and cut the sheet into round discs about 6 cm in diameter. Put a teaspoonful of the pumpkin mixture in the middle of every disc, fold in two, and with a fork press around the edge to seal.

Bring to the boil a saucepan of salted water with 2 tablespoons of oil. When the water is boiling briskly put in the tortellini, a few at a time, keeping the water boiling. Boil the tortellini until al dente. Drain and arrange the tortellini in layers, in a hot serving dish, liberally sprinkling melted butter and grated Parmesan cheese between layers.

Serves 6

Ravioli with Brains

Ravioli with brains are served either boiled in meat or chicken soup, in which case they are served with the soup or, boiled in salted water and served with tomato sauce.

If the ravioli are to be served with tomato sauce the quantities, as given in the recipe, should be proportionally increased.

INGREDIENTS:

> *Pasta:*
> 400 *g plain flour*
> 4 *eggs*
> 1-2 *tablespoons water*
>
> *Filling:*
> 400 *g brains (lamb or veal)*
> 1 *egg*
> *freshly ground pepper*
> *salt*

Under slowly running cold water clean the brains thoroughly, removing all the skin.

Put the brains into a small saucepan, cover with water and simmer for about 15 minutes. Lift the brains out of the water, and put them into a mixing bowl. Mash the brains with a fork, at the same time adding the oil, salt, pepper and one egg.

With the flour, 4 eggs, a pinch of salt and, if required, a tablespoon or two of water, prepare the dough.

Roll the dough out into a thin sheet, and cut into 3 cm squares. Put a teaspoonful of the brain mixture in the middle of each square and fold each square in half diagonally so as to form triangles. Then pinch the sides of the triangles with thumb and forefinger to close firmly.

Editor's note: According to some sources, this was a dish served at Ros Ha'shanah. The reason for that is a play on words: 'rosh' is the Hebrew for 'head', so brains are a suitable food to celebrate the 'head' of the New Year. For the same reason, it is common among Sephardic Jews to serve a whole fish, with its head intact.

Serves 6–8

Zia Lea's Ravioli

Ravioli or cappelletti can be served boiled in soup, usually a beef or chicken soup is used, or boiled in salted water like any other pasta, and served with a tomato sauce. However, if served with tomato sauce the quantities, as given in the recipe, should be proportionally increased.

INGREDIENTS:

Pasta:
500 *g plain flour*
   1 *tablespoon water*
   5 *eggs*
     pinch of salt

Filling:
150 *g lean veal*
      or
      chicken breast
150 *g brains*
 30 *g veal marrow*
  1 *small onion*
  2 *egg yolks*
      grated nutmeg
      freshly ground pepper
      salt

Prepare the pasta as usual. When ready roll it out into a thin sheet, and cut into round shapes of about 5 cm diameter.

Clean the brains under cold running water and boil in a little salted water, drain and let it cool.

Boil the veal with the onion until very tender, then season with salt and pepper. Finely mince the veal together with the boiled brains, marrow, egg yolks, salt, pepper and nutmeg.

Put a spoonful of the filling in each round piece of pasta, fold the pasta in two, shaping it into half moons and pinching it closed with your fingers, or take the two opposite sides of the half moon, lift them and pinch them together, and you will have the classical Cappelletti.

Serves 6–8

Rice

Rice is a very popular first-course dish in the Italian kitchen, be it in the Jewish kitchen or in any other. Rice cooked or served together with either vegetables, meat or poultry is usually called risotto. Most regions, and indeed most cooks, have a favourite risotto dish, hence there are countless variations in the preparation of risotto.

As the name risotto implies, rice is the only ingredient common to all risotto dishes. However, there are variations even in the choice of rise used to prepare risotto.

Because the texture of a good risotto should be that of a very thick creamed soup, the rice must be cooked until it is very soft and gluggy, so that it can better absorb the flavours of the ingredients used to create the end result.

The best and easiest way to ensure the glutinous result is to use Italian superfine rice. There are, of course, many varieties and one of the best, the Riso Superfino Arborio, is readily available in many supermarkets.

When rice is used in a soup too, it is often cooked until it releases the gluten that gives the soup a creamy texture.

Sabbath Rice

This Sabbath Rice or Pilaf was originally prepared on Friday and left in the oven at a heat so low that the rice remains hot, without sticking or disintegrating, until needed on Sabbath. I am sorry to say that this method does not work in my oven, nor in several other ovens that I have tried. Every time that I have followed the recipe, the rice was delicious when ready but, after a night in the oven at the lowest temperature possible, it became a very tasty glue. It works, however, as an everyday dish.

INGREDIENTS:

> *500 g rice*
> *1 litre chicken or meat stock, hot*
> *½ cup oil*
> *or*
> *goose fat*
> *pinch of saffron*
> *salt*
> *freshly ground pepper*

Preheat the oven to 350°F or 180°C.

In a 2-litre casserole heat the oil, add the rice and stir fry until the rice is lightly browned. Add all the hot stock at once, add the salt, pepper and saffron, stir and cover the casserole with a tightly fitting lid, and bake for 20 minutes.

An alternative way of cooking Pilaf:

Begin cooking the same way as before, but once the rice is golden brown add the boiling broth gradually and, keeping the rice boiling briskly, stir frequently.

When the rice is half cooked, add the saffron and salt to taste, and continue to cook until al dente. Then take the rice off the flame, cover it, and let it absorb all the remaining soup.

Serve with mushrooms, peas or other vegetables in season.

Serves 6

Turkish Rice

Turkish rice was a very popular dish in my Italian family but I learned to prepare it in Tel Aviv. I remember the first time I was given a compliment for my cooking. It was in Tel Aviv during the Tsena (rationing) when each grain of rice was precious. We had vegetable soup, rice and fried eggplant, and, one dish at a time, I cooked the meal on our single Primus, in the corner of our room that did kitchen duty.

Mama had horded our rations because her cousin, my Aunt Olga Alt, was coming to dinner. When Aunt Olga tasted the rice she told me that a young girl who cooked rice as I have done was going to be a very good cook! I don't know about the 'very good cook' part, but I do know that it was since that day that I enjoyed cooking and found that creating dishes with very limited ingredients really was fun.

INGREDIENTS:

> 1 *cup rice*
> 2 *cups cold water*
> 2 *tablespoons olive oil*
>   *salt*
>   *freshly ground pepper*

Heat the oil in a small saucepan and when it is very hot add the rice. Stir briskly with a wooden spoon until all the rice is coated and light golden.

Add the salt and pepper and stir once more, then add all the cold water. Once the water is added do not stir the rice again but cover the saucepan and lower the flame to the minimum possible and allow to simmer very slowly until all the water is absorbed.

Rice with Raisins

This is a very old Venetian recipe and is very popular with children. Nonna Rina often served it when grandchildren came to lunch. The children loved to look for the raisins and would pile them on to one side of the plate while eating the rice. When all the rice was gone, the raisins were counted to see who had the most. There were no prizes at the end of the game but it was a lovely way to encourage the poor eaters.

INGREDIENTS:

> 2½ *cups rice*
> 100 *g raisins*
>   5 *cups hot meat stock*
>   5 *tablespoons olive oil*
>   1 *tablespoons chopped parsley*
>   1 *clove crushed garlic*
>   *freshly ground pepper*
>   *pinch of salt*

In a 2-litre saucepan fry the garlic and parsley, discarding the garlic as soon as it is golden brown.

Add the raisins and stir fry for one minute, then add the rice and stir until the rice is well coated with oil before slowly pouring in the boiling soup.

Season with salt and pepper, cover and cook over a very low flame, stirring occasionally, until all the soup is absorbed.

Editor's note: The use of raisins in a savory dish is strange to most modern tastes, but it usually denotes an ancient recipe. This was probably an Arab dish in origin.

Serves 6

Eggplant Risotto

The texture of this dish is mushy and the looks are nothing to write home about. However, the taste is delicious.

INGREDIENTS:
- *600 g rice*
- *600 g eggplants*
- *½ cup olive oil*
- *5 cups beef stock*
- *2 tablespoons chopped parsley*
- *1 clove crushed garlic*
- *freshly ground pepper*
- *salt*

Cut the eggplants into chunks.

In a frying pan heat the oil, add the eggplant with the garlic and parsley, salt and pepper and, stirring frequently, fry slowly on a low flame, until the eggplant is so soft that is is practically puréed.

Transfer the eggplant into a saucepan, add the stock and bring it to the boil, then add the rice and, mixing it well into the eggplant, cook on a medium flame for about 10 to 12 minutes.

Add the stock and continue to cook slowly until all the stock is absorbed and the rice is ready. Stir often or it will stick to the bottom of the pan.

Serves 6–8

Polenta

Polenta is the name of the maize meal or coarse flour that polenta dishes are prepared with. In Veneto (the region from Padova to Trieste), polenta mostly replaces pasta as a first course, and is often used instead of bread. As a first course polenta is served with the same variation of sauces and condiments as pasta.

Polenta should be cooked in a heavy saucepan with a long handle to make it easier to keep the saucepan on the fire when mixing it. I was told that there are four rules one must follow to prepare a good polenta:

a. the water must be boiling briskly;
b. three tablespoons of olive oil must be poured into the water;
c. the polenta must 'rain' slowly into the water;
d. one must begin to stir when the first grain touches the boiling water and continue to stir uninterrupted for about twenty minutes.

But now it is easy to cook polenta for there are various brands on the market that do not need to be stirred and cooked so long, and have easy instructions on the packets. In the past I found it rather difficult to slowly pour polenta into boiling water and stir it without dislodging the saucepan.

Another old rule is that cold polenta should always be cut with a wire and not with a knife.

INGREDIENTS:

> *500 g polenta*
> *3 tablespoons olive oil*
> *2–3 litres water*
> *salt*

Bring the water to the boil, add the oil and, very slowly, so that the water does not stop boiling, pour in the polenta.

Stir continuously for 20–30 minutes or until the polenta is al dente.

Serve hot with a sauce or ragu, or cold instead of bread.

Serves 6–8

Carmelina's Meat Soup

Carmelina was for many years the factotum in my friend Lidia's family. Carmelina was a wonderful cook and, although she was not Jewish, having lived with Lidia for so many years, she became a veritable treasure-trove of 'do's' and 'don'ts' in the Jewish kitchen.

This is a very nourishing soup. Carmelina used to prepare it for convalescents of all ages in the whole family.

INGREDIENTS:

    1 kg soup meat
    soup bones
  300 g rice
    2 thinly sliced carrots
    1 finely chopped parsnip
    1 finely chopped onion
    2 finely chopped celery stalks
    finely chopped parsley
 4–5 tablespoons olive oil
    2 egg yolks
    juice of 1 lemon
    freshly ground pepper
    salt

The soup can be prepared in advance and reheated when needed but, to avoid curdling, the egg and lemon mixture must be added only when you are ready to serve.

Heat the oil in a saucepan until it is hot then add the onions and stir fry. When the onion is transparent add the carrots, parsnip and celery and continue to stir fry for 5 minutes.

Season with salt and pepper. Add the meat and the bones and cover with cold water. Bring to the boil, cover the saucepan, lower the heat and continue to simmer slowly until the meat is tender.

When the soup is ready remove the saucepan from the flame. Strain the soup, remove the meat and the bones, but return the vegetables to the soup. The meat can be used for another dish or finely chopped and returned to the soup.

Return the soup to the flame and bring to the boil, add the rice, stir, cover the saucepan and continue to boil very slowly, stirring occasionally so that the rice does not stick, until the rice is al dente.

When the rice is ready remove the saucepan from the flame. Put the two egg yolks and the lemon juice into a tureen and whisk lightly until blended then, whilst continuing to whisk the egg and lemon mixture, with a ladle pour the hot soup slowly over the egg and lemon mixture.

Serve hot, with chopped parsley sprinkled on each individual serving.

Serves 6–8

Creamed Chicken and Rice Soup

There is no cream in this soup, of course, but the rice gives it a creamy texture. It is a very practical recipe because it can be made in advance and can be served either hot or cold.

INGREDIENTS:

> *1.2 kg chicken*
> *4 tablespoons rice (preferably Italian Arborio)*
> *1 small onion*
> *1 small carrot*
> *1 small leek*
> *1 small celery stick*
> *1 clove (optional)*
> *freshly ground pepper*
> *salt*

Put the chicken into a saucepan with 3 litres of cold water, bring to the boil and skim off the froth as it forms on the surface.

When the soup is clear add the rice and cook until very soft.

With white kitchen string, tie the vegetables into a bunch and put the bunch of vegetables into the soup so that the string remains hanging over the rim of the saucepan for easy removal.

Season with salt and pepper, cover, lower the flame to simmer, stirring frequently.

When the chicken is tender remove it from the soup and bone it carefully.

Remove the vegetables from the soup and discard them. Strain the soup and set the broth aside.

Put the rice with the chicken pieces and a little of the broth through a sieve or purée in the food processor. When the purée is smooth, dilute it with the remaining broth, garnish with chopped parsley and serve either hot or cold, depending on the season of the year.

Serves 6

Pea Soup with Rice

I was given this recipe by a friend who had it from her grandmother and who assured me that it is a Italian-Jewish recipe. However, I remember well that my mother prepared this soup every spring, as soon as the first peas of the season were on the market. The only difference is that the Italian version of the soup is thicker than my mother's version. Who knows, maybe the Venetian Doges made this dish popular, too.

INGREDIENTS:

> 1 *kg peas, for this recipe the peas must be very fresh and young*
>   *as the pods are used, too*
> 500 *g rice*
> 4 *tablespoons olive oil*
> 2 *tablespoons chopped parsley*
> 1 *small onion whole*
> 1 *finely chopped small onion*
> 1 *small celery stalk*
> 1 *medium carrot*
>   *freshly ground pepper*
>   *salt*

Shell the peas, wash the pods well, place the pods into a saucepan together with the celery, carrot, onion and a pinch of salt, add enough water to cover, and boil slowly for about 40 to 45 minutes.

Drain the vegetable stock into a bowl and reserve. Put all the vegetables through a vegetable sieve, or purée in the food processor and return the vegetable purée to the stock. If you use a sieve, discard what is left of the pea pods.

In another saucepan heat the oil, add the peas with the chopped onion and parsley, and stir fry until lightly browned, then add enough water to cover and continue to simmer.

When the peas are tender, add the rice and stir until well mixed, then slowly add the vegetable purée, bring to the boil and simmer, covered, until the rice is ready (about 15 to 20 minutes).

Editor's note: This is a soup version of risi e bisi, a Venetian speciality traditionally served on 25 April, the Feast Day of San Marco, the patron saint of Venice. The peas were the sweet and tender first peas of the season. Perhaps this soup version came about because it was not quite appropriate to serve a dish that belonged so clearly to the Christian calendar.

Serves 6

Chick Pea Broth

This broth is a very old recipe stemming from Rome, but popular in all of Italy. When Nonna Rina was young, 'every good housewife' made her own kosher salami. These salamis were prepared with yearling beef, veal, goose or turkey, using either one type of meat or a mixture of several. The meat was cut into very thin slivers which were called 'pennerelli'. The pennerelli that were left over after the salami was made were used for this very tasty broth.

As this broth is a very filling first course, it is usually followed only by a dish of freshly steamed vegetables, and fresh fruit.

INGREDIENTS:

500 g chick peas
400 g pennerelli or
   yearling gravy beef
   1 tablespoon tomato paste
   2 tablespoons olive oil
   1 onion
   freshly ground pepper
   salt

Put all the ingredients into a stock pot, cover with cold water, bring to the boil and cover. Lower the heat and boil very slowly, for at least three hours.

Check occasionally to see if additional water is needed. If so, add boiling water.

Keep in mind that both the chick peas and the meat should be overcooked, and the broth should be very thick.

Serves 6

Potato Soup

This is a soup with a difference. Nonna Rina called it a potato soup that, unlike any other potato soup, can be served on festive occasions.

INGREDIENTS:

>   1 *kg potatoes*
>   3 *tablespoons bread crumbs*
>   3 *tablespoons chopped parsley*
>   1 *teaspoon grated nutmeg*
>   5 *eggs*
>   *freshly ground pepper*
>   *salt*
>   *enough chicken or beef stock to serve 6, taking into account that the potatoes will absorb a considerable amount of the stock*

Scrub the potatoes and boil with the skin until they are tender, then drain and peel them, put them into a mixing bowl and let them cool. When the potatoes are cold, add the eggs together with all the other ingredients and knead until well amalgamated. Bring the soup to the boil, cover, lower the flame and continue to simmer.

Wet your hands with cold water and press the potato mixture firmly together to form an oblong shape. Wrap the potato shape into a cheese cloth and tie the cloth at both ends and in the middle.

Uncover the soup, raise the flame and slowly lower the potato shape into the boiling soup, cover, lower the flame and continue to simmer, for one hour.

Remove the soup from the heat, carefully take the potato shape out of the soup and drain it over the soup pot, so that no soup is lost.

When no more soup oozes from the potato shape place it into a bowl, then put a plate on top of it and place a weight on top of the plate.

Let the potato shape stand under weight until it is quite cold, then carefully remove the cheese cloth and cut the potato shape into small cubes.

Return the soup to the heat and bring it to the boil, and when it boils briskly add the potato cubes and continue to boil for 5 minutes before serving.

Serves 6

Soup with Meatballs

In my Italian family in Naples meatballs in a good strong chicken soup are often served to convalescents, particulary children and the elderly. The elderly find the meatballs easy to digest, whilst children like fishing for the little balls. When my son Michael was a toddler, I used to mix a little steamed, mashed spinach into the meatball mixture, and the 'Soup with Green Balls' became a favourite dish.

INGREDIENTS:

> *Soup:*
> *soup bones*
> 1 *small brown onion*
> 1 *carrot*
> 1 *celery stalk*
>
> *Meatballs:*
> 600 *g finely minced topside or chicken*
> *freshly ground pepper*
> *salt*

Prepare the soup with the meat bones and vegetables, or use any other meat or chicken soup.

When the soup is ready, strain and discard the bones and vegetables, return the clear soup to the saucepan and keep it on the boil.

Combine the minced meat with the salt and pepper, mix and make little meat balls, each the size of a walnut.

Drop the meatballs into the soup and continue to boil slowly over a low flame for 30 minutes.

Serves 6

Pasta e Fagioli con Luganega

In this recipe the beans are puréed, which makes it rather unusual.

'Pasta e Fagioli' is an old, and very popular dish in Italy, and in the Italian Jewish kitchen, one of the traditional Sabbath dishes. In Venice, Donna Rachele, an ancient, rotund little lady who took her cooking very seriously—although in her late eighties when I knew her—still insisted on preparing the soup herself. Although, she told me, her daughter and granddaughters were good cooks after all she has taught them herself, she did not trust them with the preparation of 'her' Pasta e Fagioli. Only when she cooked it herself was it a dish 'fit for a Doge'.

INGREDIENTS:

- 300 g mezzi tubetti
- 500 g beans of your choice (traditionally dark beans are used for all pasta e fagioli dishes)
- 5 tablespoons olive oil
- 2 finely chopped onions
- 1 finely chopped carrot
- 1 finely chopped celery stalk
  freshly ground pepper
  salt
- 200 g luganega (see recipe on page 115)

In a saucepan heat part of the oil. When the oil is hot add the vegetables, stir fry until all the vegetables are lightly browned.

Add the beans and the luganega to the vegetables with enough cold water to reach about twice the height of the ingredients. Cover the saucepan, and bring to the boil. Lower the flame to minimum and continue to simmer for at least 2 hours.

Turn off the heat. Take the luganega out of the soup and allow it to rest for a while. In the meantime strain the soup into another saucepan and return it to a low flame.

Reserve a cupful of whole beans. Purée the remaining beans and vegetables in the food processor. Cut the luganega into coarse pieces and return it to the soup together with the vegetable purée and the whole beans.

Bring to the boil, stirring frequently. Add the pasta and, stirring very frequently, continue to boil briskly until the pasta is al dente.

If needed, whilst still cooking, add a little boiling water. The soup should be thick, but not a heavy paste.

When the pasta is al dente and the soup is ready to be served, stir in the remaining oil.

Serves 6

Intermediate Courses
and Eggs

Pastry for Pasticci

Buricche and Pasticci are baked shapes of pastry with a variety of filling.

The pastry is simple and easy to make, there is practically nothing that can go wrong. It was a favourite of Zia Tilde's. She had it ready in no time at all and whilst the pastry rested she prepared whatever filling she fancied at the time. Zia Emma's Virginia and Zia Tilde were in a perennial competition with each other, always inventing new fillings for the pasticci.

Editor's note: Buricche were very much a Jewish dish, according to Edda Servi Machlin ('The Classic Cuisine of the Italian Jews'), who said that some people believed their name came from the Spanish word for donkey (burro) since they looked like donkey's ears. It is more likely that the name is a variant of borek, the Turkish for a filled pastry. But perhaps there is something in the association of the dish with Spain, since these savory pastries are most popular with Sephardim, those Jews

45

who moved eastwards from Spain, and they appear in Sephardi cooking from Turkey, Greece and Yugoslavia. There they are known as borekas. In Lebanon, Syria and Egypt, similar pastries are known as sanbusak.

INGREDIENTS:

> *1 cup olive oil*
> *1 cup water*
> *plain flour*
> *pinch of salt*

Prepare some flour in a large mixing bowl keeping more flour handy to be used if needed. Make a hollow in the middle of the flour.

In a small saucepan warm the water with the oil and a pinch of salt. When the water is quite warm pour it into the middle of the hollow in the flour and, adding more flour if necessary, knead into a smooth, firm ball of pastry.

Cover the pastry with a kitchen towel and allow it to rest for about half an hour, then flatten the pastry with a rolling pin and roll it out into a thin sheet, about 5 millimetres or less.

Remember to keep the rolling pin and working surface well floured.

Cut the pastry into round shapes with a sharp biscuit cutter or cut into squares with a sharp knife.

Put the filling of your choice in the middle of the shapes, fold each shape in two and pinch firmly all around to close securely, and bake on a baking tray sprinkled with flour.

Puff Pastry for Pasticci

The first time I followed this recipe I found the instructions to 'work the ingredients into a smooth dough, the dough must be neither too soft nor too hard', very intriguing! I wondered what exactly that meant.

Well, I found out. It means exactly what the recipe says: smooth and pliable. It is also exasperating because, as the dough is being rolled it continues to retract and returns to its original size. It becomes a contest between the cook and the dough.

If you are in a hurry go out and buy some ready made puff pastry but, if you decide to make the pastry yourself, remember that puff pastry, when baked and ready to be served must be:

a. manipulated with care to avoid breakage
b. cut with either a very sharp bread knife or an electric knife to avoid squashing the edges

INGREDIENTS:

> 200 g plain flour
> 150 g goose fat, ghee
>   or
>   margarine
>   ½ cup tepid water
>   1 tablespoon grappa or brandy
>   pinch of salt

Put the flour with the water, grappa or brandy, salt and 1 teaspoon of the fat into a large bowl and mix until the pastry is smooth and pliable, then put the pastry on a working surface sprinkled with flour and, continue to knead until the dough detaches easily from the surface and from the hands, cover the pastry with a damp cloth and allow it to rest for half an hour.

Uncover and, continuing to work on a flat surface, press the dough firmly with the palm of your hand until you have a flat rectangle about 1 centimetre thick.

Cut the remaining fat into small pieces, sprinkle with flour and spread over one half of the dough, then fold the second half of the pastry over the fat, as if you were making a parcel.

Wrap the folded pastry with a damp cloth and allow it to rest in the fridge for half an hour.

Sprinkle the working surface with flour, remove the pastry from the cloth and, using a rolling pin in an even, up-and-down motion, roll the pastry until it is about 1 centimetre thick.

Whilst rolling the pastry take care not to allow any of the pieces of fat to escape.

Fold the pastry into three, folding first the bottom third upwards, then the top third over it, so that you have three even layers sitting on top of each other.

Turn the folded pastry once to the right so that the horizontal fold becomes vertical and roll out again, as you did before, until it is again 1 centimetre thick.

Fold the pastry twice to make three even layers sitting on top of each other, as you did before. Wrap the folded pastry into the damp cloth and allow to rest in a cool place for another half an hour.

Repeat this procedure two more times, allowing the pastry to rest for half an hour between each procedure.

Work the same way each time: place the pastry onto the working surface with the rolling pin at right angles to the fold, and turn once to the right.

The fat must not be allowed to harden, melt, or become amalgamated with the pastry, it must form a layer between the layers of pastry.

Keep the pastry and the rolling pin well sprinkled with flour, roll out the pastry into a thin sheet, cut into round shapes with a sharp biscuit cutter or cut it into squares with a sharp knife.

Put the filling of your choice in the middle of the shapes, fold each shape in two and pinch firmly all around to close securely.

Bake on a baking tray sprinkled with flour.

Editor's note: The pastry can also be made with beef marrow, which appears to be uniquely Italian-Jewish. It is not common, and not much to modern tastes.

Puff Pastry with Beef Marrow

Using marrow definitely gives the pastry a 'different' taste, however I can not say that I like it very much. I include it here only for the sake of interest because I find it rather unusual. It is the only recipe that I ever came across that uses beef marrow instead of chicken or goose fat.

Editor's note: This looks like another uniquely Italian-Jewish recipe. I have found bone marrow as a variant ingredient for oil or fat in another Italian Jewish cookbook, but nowhere else.

INGREDIENTS:

    300 g beef marrow
      3 tablespoons water
        plain flour
        salt

Place the marrow into a bowl full of cold water and break it up until it is white and free of any trace of blood, drain and press together with your hands to form a ball.

Weigh the marrow and add to the marrow an equal amount of flour, the water and a pinch of salt.

Knead until you have a smooth dough then, without adding more fat, work the dough as the puff pastry in the previous recipe, repeating the procedure eight times with ten-minute rest periods.

Roll the dough into a 5-millimetre-thick sheet.

Cut into round shapes with a sharp biscuit cutter, or with a sharp knife cut the dough into squares, put the filling of your choice in the middle of the shapes, and press firmly around the filling to close securely.

Bake on a floured baking tray.

Pasta Brisé

Pasta Brisé is also widely used for sweets. It is simple to prepare and need not be altered for use with sweet fillings.

INGREDIENTS:

> 150 g plain flour
> 75 g goose fat or ghee
> 2-3 tablespoons cold water
> pinch of salt

Sprinkle the working surface with flour, put the flour on the working surface then put the fat on top of the flour and rub together.

When the pastry has crumbled, add the salt then, slowly adding the water, knead into a softish, pliable ball. Cover with a napkin and allow to rest for half an hour.

After half an hour roll the pastry into a 5-millimetre-thin sheet. Cut into round shapes with a sharp biscuit cutter, or cut into squares with a sharp knife.

Put the filling of your choice in the middle of each shape, fold each shape in two and pinch firmly all around to close securely.

Bake on a baking tray sprinkled with flour.

Fillings for Pasticci

Pasticci (the smaller ones are known as pasticcini) are very like buricche.

The variety of fillings used for pasticci is limited only by the cook's imagination. Practically anything and everything can be combined into a filling. I have included recipes for the fillings which are considered typically Italian-Jewish.

INGREDIENTS:

> *for each 100 g of meat you will need:*
> 2 *tablespoons chopped onion*
> 1 *slice of stale white bread*
>   *a little olive oil (optional)*
> 1 *egg*
>   *stock*
>   *freshly ground pepper*
>   *salt*

Put the meat, onion, oil, salt and pepper into a small saucepan, cover with water and cook on a low flame until the meat is tender and all the water has evaporated.

Remove from the flame and allow to cool.

Soak the bread in stock, squeeze it dry.

Put the meat, onions and bread through the mincer, add the eggs, season with salt and pepper and mix until well amalgamated.

Meat Filling with Left-overs

INGREDIENTS:

> *for each 200 g of cooked meat you will need:*
> 1 *tablespoon chopped onion*
> 1 *slice stale white bread*
>   *a little olive oil (optional)*
> 1 *egg*
>   *freshly ground pepper*
>   *salt*

Mince the meat with the onion, add the eggs and mix together, taste for salt and pepper.

Chicken and Liver Filling

INGREDIENTS:

> 200 g minced chicken breast
> 1 cup chicken stock
> 3 tablespoons olive oil
> 2 chicken livers
> 2 eggs
> 2 hard-boiled eggs
> freshly ground pepper
> salt

Heat the oil in a small saucepan, add the minced chicken breast and stir fry until brown, add the stock and simmer until the chicken is tender and the stock has evaporated.

Put the chicken liver into a frying pan with a little oil and fry until brown, remove from the flame and mince together with the breasts, hard-boiled eggs, salt and pepper.

Combine all the ingredients and mix until well amalgamated.

Fish Filling

Mince any cooked, boned fish with a couple of anchovy fillets.

Put the mixture into a mixing bowl, add a couple of egg yolks (it also works well with egg whites instead of yolks), season with salt and pepper and the fish filling is ready.

Eggplant Filling

With this filling, the buricche are also very nice if fried instead of baked.

INGREDIENTS:

> 500 g finely chopped eggplant
> 200 g peeled, chopped tomatoes
>   3 tablespoons chopped parsley
>   1 large chopped onion
>   1 cup olive oil
>   freshly ground pepper
>   salt

Heat the oil in a saucepan, add the onion and fry. When the onion is brown add the eggplant, tomatoes, salt and pepper and simmer slowly until the vegetables are overcooked and can be mashed with a fork.

Place the mashed vegetables into a sieve and allow to drain while you prepare the pastry.

Editor's note: More evidence of the Sephardic presence in Italy in this eggplant filling, which is regarded as a Sephardic filling in Middle-Eastern cooking, too. Fried, these are really the same as sanbusak.

Pasticcini with Chicken

Pasticcini are only a smaller version of pasticci and the pastries and fillings are interchangeable.

INGREDIENTS:

> *Pastry:*
> 200 g plain flour
>   1 cup olive oil
>   1 tablespoon olive oil
>   2 eggs
>   salt

Filling:
400 *g boiled minced chicken breast*
  2 *slices crustless white bread*
  ½ *teaspoon grated nutmeg*
    freshly ground pepper
    salt

Pastry:

Mix the flour with the oil, a pinch of salt and the eggs, knead until smooth, then form a ball, cover it with a damp cloth and allow it to rest in a cool place for half an hour.

Divide the pastry into six equal pieces and roll out each piece of pastry until it is about 20 centimetres in diameter and 2 centimetres thick.

Sprinkle the working surface with flour. Put a piece of the rolled out dough on the working surface and brush the top surface of the pastry liberally with oil.

Place the second piece of pastry on top and brush it with oil. Continue until all six pieces are oiled and layered on top of each other but do not oil the top layer, sprinkle that with flour.

With a rolling pin flatten the stack of pastry, rolling first in one direction then, giving it half a turn, in the other direction.

Allow the pastry to rest for ten minutes then continue to roll, turning the pastry always in the same direction, until it is no more than 4 millimetres thick.

Cut the shapes with a sharp biscuit cutter, put the filling in the middle of the shapes, fold each pastry round in half and close either by pinching it with your fingers or by pressing firmly with the prongs of a fork.

Filling:

Soak the bread in stock, squeeze dry, add the minced chicken breast and the seasoning and mix well together.

Melina di Pasta Limpada

An old Venetian pastry recipe. Baked in a serving dish and served with a fresh side salad, the melina is a very nice luncheon dish.

INGREDIENTS:

400 g plain flour
100 g castor sugar (used only for sweet fillings)
2 tablespoons olive oil
2 eggs

Combine all the ingredients and knead until smooth, divide the pastry in half and roll it out until you have two sheets, each about 1 centimetre thick.

Place one sheet of pastry into an oiled, round baking tin so that it covers the sides and overlaps the top of the tin.

Preheat the oven to medium heat, 350°F, 180°C.

Fill with the filling of your choice (fillings for buricche are often used). Cover with the second sheet of pastry and, with your fingers, pinch the top and bottom sheets together.

With a needle or the point of a sharp knife, pierce two diagonal lines of tiny holes across the top of the pastry.

Bake for 45 minutes or until the pastry is golden brown.

Editor's note: I cannot find the word melina anywhere else. But there is a dish called 'mina', which is a pie that was made by Sephardic Jews from Turkey and Greece during Passover, with a layer of matza top and bottom, like the pasta layers in the pie here. I cannot say if the two names and two dishes have a common ancestry.

Brioche with Ragù

The brioche is a practical and delicious way to disguise left-overs. It is also a practical lunch or supper dish that can be prepared in advance.

INGREDIENTS:

> *Pastry:*
> 40 g baker's yeast
> 250 g plain flour
> 3 tablespoons olive oil
> 4 tablespoons stock at body temperature
> 1 egg
>
> *Filling:*
> 150 g sliced mushrooms
> 2 cups ragù (see page 108)
> salt and pepper

Oil a deep baking dish and sprinkle the bottom and sides with bread crumbs.

In a mixing bowl combine the yeast with the stock, add the egg, salt, oil and flour and mix with a wooden spoon, until the pastry is soft but not runny.

Divide the pastry in half and roll it out.

Preheat the oven to medium heat, 400°F, 200°C.

Carefully transfer one sheet of pastry into the tin, without disturbing the bread crumbs, distribute the mushrooms evenly over the dough, pour the ragù over the mushrooms and cover with the other sheet of pastry.

With your fingers pinch the top and the bottom pastries together all around and, with a needle or with the point of a sharp knife, pierce two diagonal lines of tiny holes across the top of the pastry.

Bake for 40 minutes or until the pastry is golden brown.

Serves 6

Eggs in Bread Sauce

Eggs in bread sauce are a lovely way to serve eggs for breakfast, although no one ate eggs for breakfast in Napoli. This dish was usually served for supper.

Be careful with the temperature of the plates. The serving plates must be warmed but do not heat them or the eggs will continue to cook and harden.

Timing is also important, although it is simple to prepare the sauce in advance and cook the eggs only when everybody is already at the table.

When we had visitors Nonna Rina never served this dish, nor did she serve omelettes, for the simple reason that the large dining room was 10 metres down the corridor from the kitchen and no omelette could survive the trip.

INGREDIENTS:

> 30 g capers
> 1 tablespoon white vinegar
> 4 tablespoons olive oil
> 6 eggs
> 1 stale bread roll
> 4 sprigs parsley
> 1 garlic clove
>   freshly ground pepper
>   salt

Sauce:
  Soak the bread in water with a drop of vinegar, and squeeze dry.
  Put the bread, capers, parsley, oil and pepper into the food processor and mince until the sauce is thick and smooth.

Eggs:
  Bring to the boil a shallow saucepan full of water, with one tablespoon of vinegar, and a little salt and, when the water boils, lower the heat and keep the water boiling slowly.
  Crack an egg into a cup and, holding the cup on the surface of the water, slowly, without breaking the yolk, slide the egg into the boiling water. After the third egg is put into the water the first egg should

be ready to be removed. The egg white should be firmly set and the yolk should no longer quiver.

Remove the eggs with a slotted spoon, one at a time, and place them on warmed, individual serving dishes, cover with the sauce and serve.

Serves 6

Eggs in the Nest

In the recipe I have given the instructions exactly as I received them from Virginia, however, every time I tried to follow the instructions to the letter, the egg yolks just kept sliding all over the place and it was very difficult to retrieve the yolks without breaking them.

I find it much simpler to reverse the order of Virginia's instructions and place the beaten egg white on the tongue first, then make a well in the middle of the egg white, and slide the yolk into the well.

I also like to substitute a slice of cheese for the slice of tongue.

INGREDIENTS:

> *6 eggs*
> *6 slices of bread*
> *6 slices of pickled veal tongue*
> *freshly ground pepper*
> *salt*

Preheat the oven to 350°F, 180°C.

Arrange the bread slices, next to each other, in a shallow ovenproof serving dish and put a slice of tongue on each slice of bread, separate the eggs and put one egg yolk in the centre of each slice of tongue.

Beat the egg whites with a pinch of salt until stiff, then, with a spoon, arrange the beaten egg whites around each egg yolk forming small peaks, put a drop of oil on each egg yolk.

Bake until the egg whites become golden brown.

Serves 6

Eggs in Tomato Sauce

Instead of beating the eggs first, as the recipe says, I prefer to transfer the sauce to a shallow serving dish that can be put on the cooking top, crack the eggs one at a time, and slide them whole into the tomato sauce, then cover the pan and simmer until the eggs are cooked but not hard.

I remember cooking the eggs my way and serving the dish when Zia Tilde was visiting from Africa. She was furious because I dared to alter 'her recipe!'

INGREDIENTS:

> 500 *g ripe, peeled tomatoes, roughly chopped*
> 5 *tablespoons olive oil*
> 7 *eggs*
> 1 *crushed garlic clove*
> *pinch of hot chilli*
> *salt*

Heat the oil in a saucepan, add the garlic and fry until the garlic is brown then discard it. Add the tomatoes, salt and chilli to the hot oil and simmer slowly until it becomes a thick sauce.

In a mixing bowl beat the eggs with a fork or a whisk until frothy.

When you are ready to serve pour the beaten eggs into the boiling tomato sauce, lower the heat and continue to simmer, stirring continuously, until the eggs have set.

Serves 6

Eggs in Tomato and Chilli Sauce

Very often a couple of hot chillies are added to the tomato sauce.

INGREDIENTS:

500 g ripe, peeled chopped tomatoes
250 g finely chopped green peppers
  5 tablespoons olive oil
  6 eggs
  2 sliced onions
  2 hot chillies
  2 crushed garlic cloves
    freshly ground pepper
    salt

Heat the oil in a large, deep frying pan, add the onion with a tablespoon of water and simmer until the water evaporates and the onion is brown. Add the tomatoes and continue to simmer, over a low heat, for about 15 minutes, then add the peppers, garlic and pepper and continue to simmer, covered, for about 1 hour.

Preheat the oven to 350°F, 180°C.

When you are ready to serve, pour the sauce into a preheated wide and shallow ovenproof serving dish.

With a wooden spoon, make six hollows in the sauce and gently slide an egg into each hollow, cover and continue to simmer for another ten minutes or until the egg whites are firmly set. Serve as soon as ready.

Serves 6

Fish

When I lived in Naples, Salvatore the fishmonger still hawked his wares from house to house. In the early morning he passed our house, walking slowly, offering his wares in a melodious sing-song.

On his head he carried a wooden tub full of sea-water and a variety of fish. With one hand he steadied his load and in the other he held the scales.

Every household had—and probably still has—a basket tied to a cord long enough to reach the street when lowered from a window. In our case it was very long—we lived on the seventh floor.

When Giuseppina, the maid, heard Salvatore approaching she put an empty bowl, a note on which Nonna Rina had written the order, and the money to pay for it into the basket and lowered it to the street.

When Salvatore reached the basket he stopped, lowered his tub to the ground, chose and weighed the fish and put it in the bowl. Sometimes the fish was still alive and he had to knock it on the head before he could put it in the basket. Then he wiped his hands on a large red handkerchief, counted the money and put the right change into the basket as well, before he looked up, waved and shouted 'ciao Giuseppina'.

Giuseppina raised the basket while Salvatore hoisted his load onto his head, picked up his scales and, singing, walked on towards the next hanging basket.

Dawn found Salvatore on the pier in Mergelina, waiting for the fishing boats to return with their catch. When he had sold all the fish he could carry on his head, he returned to the pier, bought more fish and continued his rounds until late into the morning when it was too close to lunch-time to sell his wares.

Editor's note: Italian-Jewish fish cookery has a number of things in common with other styles of Jewish cooking. The first is in the kinds of fish used, since kosher fish are those which have scales and fins. So there are no recipes here for shellfish or molluscs, and none for squid or octopus. Another thing to note is the number of recipes for dishes that are to be served cold. The reason for that is related to religious observance: work (including cooking) is forbidden on the Sabbath and other festival days. If observant Jews are to eat, they need dishes that can be prepared ahead of time.

The author has a particular fondness for sardines, and tells her own story about that, so there are more sardine recipes here than in most other cookbooks.

Fish in Aspic 1

Fish in aspic is a very festive dish, served at nearly every holiday meal. Arrange slices of hard boiled eggs, alternating the eggs with sprigs of parsley, around the fish before the aspic sets, and you will have a very impressive looking dish.

INGREDIENTS:

> 1 *kg either sea bream, pike or sea carp, whole*
> 2 *tablespoons chopped parsley*
> 1 *tablespoon plain flour*
> 4 *tablespoons olive oil*
> 1 *tablespoon sultanas*
> 1 *tablespoon pine nuts*
> 1 *cup white wine vinegar*
> 500 *ml water*
> 2–3 *cloves crushed garlic*
>   *freshly ground pepper*
>   *salt*

Heat the oil with the parsley and garlic.

Coat the fish with flour, and fry in a deep pan, until the fish is golden brown on both sides. Add the water, vinegar, salt, pepper, sultanas and pine nuts, bring to the boil and continue to simmer until the liquid is reduced to one third of its original quantity.

Carefully lift the fish out of the frying pan and put it on a preheated serving dish, cover with the juices and let it cool then refrigerate.

When cold, the juices will set into aspic.

Serve refrigerated, garnished with sprigs of parsley and lemon wedges.

Serves 4

Fish in Aspic 2

For this recipe you need no extra decorations because, whilst the cooking liquid is cooling the fried vegetable pieces will float to the top, the liquid will set, and the finished dish will look very attractive.

INGREDIENTS:

1 kg firm fleshed fish, either pike, sea bream, trevally or snapper
½ cup white wine vinegar
1 cup finely chopped parsley
1 cup olive oil
1 small stalk finely chopped celery
1 small grated carrot
1 medium onion
2 bay leaves
2 cloves crushed garlic
juice of 2 lemons
freshly ground pepper
salt

Put the parsley, celery and carrot in the food processor, and chop finely, but do not allow the vegetables to disintegrate.

Put the fish into the fish kettle together with the onion, bay leaves, salt, pepper and vinegar, add enough cold water to cover the fish, cover, and bring to boil. Reduce the heat and continue to simmer very slowly, until there are only about two cups of liquid left. Take the fish out of the kettle, and allow it to cool. When cold, remove all the bones, and arrange the fish pieces on a deep serving plate, set aside.

Drain the reduced fish soup through a fine sieve and set aside.

In a small saucepan heat the oil, add the garlic and minced vegetables, season with salt and pepper, stir fry until well cooked. Discard the garlic and strain the vegetables, discarding as much oil as possible.

Return the vegetables to the saucepan, reheat and add the lemon juice and the strained fish soup, mix well, pour over the fish and let it cool.

Serves 4

Boiled Fish Alla Giudea

When cooking whole fish, remember that the fish is cooked when the eyes become white. I know it sounds ghastly, but one does get used to it, and it is a foolproof method of avoiding overcooked fish. To any food-loving Italian, overcooked fish is as devastating as overcooked pasta.

INGREDIENTS:

> *Broth*
> *(vary quantities according to the size of the fish)*
> *onion*
> *celery stalk*
> *carrot*
> *parsley*
> *bay leaf*
> *freshly ground pepper*
> *salt*

To obtain the best result with boiled fish, it is imperative to begin with the preparation of a sufficient quantity of the appropriate vegetable broth. Enough liquid must be prepared to cover the fish, so the quantity of vegetables and water to be used depends on the size of the fish. The broth can be prepared directly in the fish kettle.

Fill the fish kettle with as much water as you will need to cover the fish, add salt, pepper, onion, celery stalks, carrots, parsley, one or two bay leaves, and either half a cup of white wine vinegar, or half a cup of lemon juice. Boil for about 20 to 30 minutes, then drain, discard the vegetables and return the broth to the kettle and let it cool.

Rub the fish with sliced lemon. Lift the perforated tray out of the fish kettle and place the fish on the tray. When the soup is cold put the tray with the fish into the kettle, cover the kettle and bring to the boil slowly over a low heat, then continue to simmer as slowly as possible. Calculate the cooking time according to the size of the fish, from 15 to 20 minutes per kilo, or until the eyes are white.

Grilled Fish

Always use a whole fish for grilling and rub the fish with sliced lemon.

Leaving the head on or discarding the head is of course optional. However, the morsels of fish found at the base of the head are considered the tastiest parts of any fish.

Fish is even more delicious if cooked on the barbecue instead of under the griller. Just invert the order of brushing on the oil, salt, pepper and bread crumbs.

INGREDIENTS:

fish of your choice
olive oil
bread crumbs
chopped parsley
1 *lemon halved*
freshly ground pepper
salt

Preheat the griller, brush the griller and the upper part of the fish with oil, sprinkle with salt, pepper and bread crumbs, place under the hot griller for half the cooking time needed, calculating 15 minutes per 500 g of fish.

Turn the fish very gently, to avoid breaking it, and brush the other side of the fish with the remaining oil, salt, pepper and bread crumbs. Return to the griller.

When the fish is ready to be served, place it on a heated serving dish and sprinkle liberally with the chopped parsley.

As with all other grilled food, grilled fish should be served as soon as it is ready.

Fish Soup from Venice

This recipe was given to me in Israel by a very dear friend who came from Venice. I never cooked it in Israel—for one reason or another I never had a sufficient variety of fish to prepare it. Strangely enough the first time I ate it was in a restaurant at the Lido of Venice, at a meal offered by my brother-in-law Fulvio.

INGREDIENTS:

>   2.5 *kg assorted whole fish*
>   1 *kg peeled, seeded tomatoes*
>   3 *tablespoons finely chopped parsley*
>   ½ *cup olive oil*
>   ½ *cup dry white wine*
>   3 *cloves crushed garlic*
>   2 *small hot chillies*
>   1 *stalk sliced celery*
>   1 *medium sliced carrot*
>   1 *finely chopped onion*
>   *freshly ground pepper*
>   *salt*

Ask your fishmonger to clean the whole fish, cutting off the heads but not discarding them. (No respectable fish soup should be cooked without the fish heads.)

Put the fish and the fish heads into a saucepan with the celery, carrot and onion, a pinch of salt and enough water to reach about half way up the fish. Cover the saucepan and boil for 15 minutes.

Remove the fish from the saucepan, put it on a plate, and let the fish head continue to boil for another 15–20 minutes, then strain the soup, return the soup to the saucepan and keep it hot.

In another saucepan heat the oil, add the garlic and chillies, and as soon as the garlic becomes lightly coloured, add the wine and boil briskly until the wine evaporates, add the tomatoes, cover, lower the flame, and simmer for at least 30 minutes. Stir occasionally, and if necessary, add a little of the hot soup.

Bone the fish. Add to the tomato sauce the boned fish and the parsley, and dilute it with one or two cups of hot fish soup. Boil briskly for another 5 minutes before serving in a well warmed tureen.

Serves 6

Fish Soup from Livorno

On the page with this recipe in my recipe scrap book, I wrote that I received it from Angelina's mother. I wish I could remember who they were.

INGREDIENTS:

      2.5 kg assorted fish
      500 g peeled, seeded tomatoes
        1 cup olive oil
        ½ cup wine
        3 cloves crushed garlic
      1–2 hot chillies cut small
            finely chopped fresh ginger, optional
        6 large, thick slices of oven toasted bread, preferably white
            salt

Use as many different varieties of fish as available. The fish should be cleaned, and cut into about 4–5-cm-thick slices. The heads should be left whole.

Heat the oil in a saucepan, add the garlic, chilli and ginger. When lightly browned add the wine and let it boil until the wine evaporates. Add the tomatoes and a pinch of salt and continue to simmer for 15 minutes. Add the fish and, if necessary, a little fish stock or water, cover the saucepan, lower the heat and continue to simmer for 30 minutes.

Discard the heads.

Arrange the toast on a heated serving dish and distribute the pieces of fish on top of the toast, then pour the sauce over the fish.

Serve piping hot with a fresh side salad.

Editor's note: This is the Jewish version of cacciucco, the Tuscan coast version of fish soup. Note that it contains no shellfish, as cacciucco does.

Serves 6

Baked Hake

This dish was a speciality of Zia Tilde. During the baking the fish must be basted frequently and Zia Tilde made such a performance of it that Nonna Rina and I had a wonderful time teasing her.

The three of us used to sit in the 'salone' at one of the French windows with the view of Vesuvius and Capri. We knitted, embroidered and chatted while every few minutes Tilde jumped up and ran down the long passage to the kitchen because she did not trust Giuseppina to baste the fish.

INGREDIENTS:

1 *hake, 500–600 g*
1 *tablespoon bread crumbs*
3 *tablespoons parsley*
1 *cup dry white wine*
8 *anchovy fillets*
pinch of rosemary
olive oil
freshly ground pepper
salt (careful, anchovies are salty)

Ask your fishmonger to clean the hake, leaving it whole but discarding the head.

Preheat the oven to 350°F or 180°C.

Brush the fish on both sides with oil, roll in bread crumbs and place it in a baking dish in which you have put a few tablespoons of oil and half of the wine.

In a small saucepan heat a little oil and stir fry the anchovies with the parsley and rosemary, until the anchovies have disintegrated and amalgamated with the oil, then pour this hot sauce over the fish and bake for 1 hour. During the baking baste frequently and liberally with wine and oil.

When ready, lift the whole fish onto a heated serving dish, garnish with sprigs of parsley and serve with boiled potatoes sprinkled with chopped parsley.

Editor's note: Try this recipe with gemfish.

Serves 2–3

The Chamber Pots of Vela Luka

I truly believe that my mother's sanity was saved by the sight of the chamber pots of Vela Luka. That was the village on the island of Korcula, in Dalmatia, where we were interned during the war. At that time, the island was occupied by Italy, and the population of the village was made up of about 300 villagers and about as many interned Jewish refugees from all over Jugoslavia.

My mother and I escaped from Zagreb late in 1941. I was 13 years old. My cousin Mira Sanjina obtained false documents for us in the name of Mrs Kovac and daughter, and with these Mama and I boarded a train for Split.

It was a traumatic journey. We were terrified that we would be discovered and taken off the train since our papers were not exactly the work of a professional counterfeiter. The train was very crowded, but we had boarded hours before the scheduled departure time so that Mama had a window seat, and I was squashed between her and an old peasant woman with lots of petticoats and bundles. I was very glad of her petticoats—they kept me warm.

When the conductor came to check tickets and travelling documents, he held our papers for a long time. Mama began to shiver and groan, and just when I thought it was the end of us, the old man sitting opposite Mama stood up and placed himself between her and the conductor. He began to fuss, touching Mama's forehead, and then complaining loudly: 'The woman is sick. Good God, she is burning with fever, God only knows what illness she will give us all.' The conductor returned our papers and left the carriage quickly. The old man, glancing from Mama to me, took out a battered vacuum flask, poured something into the cup and gave it to Mama. She drank it without a word, and whatever it was, it calmed her for the rest of the journey.

When we arrived in Split, it was dark. With the old man's help, I pushed and pulled Mama and our suitcases off the train. He vanished as soon as we were on the platform, and then I realised I had to hold Mama upright. She could not stand on her own; it was as if she had turned into a rag doll.

A voice was shouting directions over a loudspeaker ordering civilian passengers to the waiting room. It was long past curfew, which meant we had to spend the night in the station's waiting room, but I knew we could not. I knew we had to reach the pier and board the ship in the dark before it left for the island of Korcula. Mama was helpless, but in the blackout I managed to get her and the suitcase around the corner of the station building.

Before we left Zagreb I had memorised the map showing the way from the railway station to the docks and the pier where our ship would be anchored. Thus, even in the dark, by counting street corners I was able to find my way.

There was no moon that night. It was very dark, cold and windy, and that protected us. The wind muffled the sound of our footsteps as we moved along the street, ducking into doorways if we saw the carabinieri. They were cold, too, busily slapping their gloved hands together for warmth rather than looking for strays like us.

Just as we reached the docks we collided with a solitary carabiniere. The fright caused me to lose my hold on Mama and she slid to the ground. As the carabiniere and I struggled to pull Mama to her feet I realised with relief that he had not called his colleague.

He whispered to us, asking what we were doing on the docks so late at night after curfew. Startled and frightened, I whispered back. I told him my father was dead (which was true), and that we had spent Christmas in town with my uncle when Mama became ill. I wanted to get her aboard the ship and take her home to our island. We had lost our travelling permit, I said, but the guard on the ship was a man from our village and he would smuggle us aboard if we reached the boat before daylight. I did not tell him that I had a gold coin ready to put into the guard's hand, and that I could only hope for the best.

The carabiniere looked at Mama and the shabby old suitcase, then nodded, picked up the case and, helping to hold Mama upright, he escorted us to the ship's ladder. He handed the suitcase to the old sailor and whispered, 'Here are your friends, help them', then disappeared.

Before the astonished sailor could say anything, I opened my fist and showed him the gold coin. He opened his mouth, then closed it, took the coin and pushed us to a hidden corner of the deck. He gestured that we were to sit on the ground, and we did. We held on to each other, cowering in the dark corner where all the winds of the seas seemed to congregate, and spent what was left of the night.

In the morning, amid the hustle and bustle of departure, Mama and I were no longer conspicuous. I found the sailor again, and for another gold coin he promised to get us safely off the ship when it docked in Vela Luka, where Mama's sister and brother-in-law and my cousin Vera were interned, and where we hoped to join them.

The old sailor kept his word. He helped me get Mama and the suitcase down the ship's ladder and onto the ground. Mama was no better. I had to hold her up while I asked a woman if she knew where our family was. She pointed to a large house on the other side of the little bay, and we set off.

I was tired, cold and hungry, and afraid, too, but the sun was shining, the village looked like a pretty postcard, the sea glittered in the sun, the woman I had spoken to was friendly, and if I could only get Mama out of her shocked lethargy, I thought all would be well with my world.

We started down the street. It seemed endless as I pulled Mama along, telling her over and over that we had made it, we were safe, we had not far to go. I was speaking more to reassure myself than her.

When we finally reached the house, I stopped and told Mama to look up at the window and perhaps she would see Aunty. We looked

up together, and what we saw suddenly pulled Mama out of her despair. We stood there, the two of us, laughing hysterically.

The house had two storeys, each storey had three windows, and on each window sill stood a row of vividly coloured chamber pots!

Much later, my uncle explained that when the refugees came to the island there was a dire shortage of cooking utensils. Soon after they had settled, Uncle discovered that an enterprising villager had bought a shipment of large chamber pots. But although there were only outside lavatories on the island, the villager found no customers. Uncle, always the successful businessman, bought all the pots and sold them among those refugees who could pay for them.

They were used for cooking. Meals were cooked in them, and fish was stored in them for the winter. We soon got used to seeing the colourful chamber pots in the kitchen and on the table, and I still believe that on that first day the sight of them in the windows saved my mother's sanity.

Fresh Anchovies or Sardines with Endive

The sardine is dark fleshed and stronger in flavour than the anchovy, however, most cooks interchange the two varieties and use the same recipe for both.

Editor's note: This dish is thought to be a speciality of Roman Jews. Roman Jewish cooking characteristically combined fish or meat with vegetables in a single dish. Italian Jewish cooking is as regional as Italian cooking. If you cannot find anchovies and do not like sardines, try it with fillets of sole. I have noted a number of recipes where sole is used for a more refined version, and sardines prepared by those who could not afford the more expensive fish.

INGREDIENTS:

>   1 *kg fresh sardines*
>   2 *kg white inner endive leaves*
>   *olive oil*
>   *freshly ground pepper*
>   *salt*

Clean and gut the sardines and remove the backbone, then rinse and drain in a colander.

Discard the hard outer leaves from the endive and remove the core, wash the endive, drain but do not dry.

In a lightly oiled baking dish, arrange alternating layers of endive and sardines—layers of endive should be at least a couple of leaves thick—beginning and ending with a triple layer of endive leaves. Sprinkle each layer with oil, salt and pepper. Cover the baking dish, pressing the food down. It will cook in its own juices, reducing the volume considerably. Cook for 15 minutes.

Uncover the baking dish and bake in a preheated oven, at 400°F or 200°C, for about 30 minutes or until there is a golden crust on top and all the juices have evaporated.

This dish can be served hot, directly from the oven or cold with a sprinkling of lemon juice.

Serves 8

Baked Anchovies or Sardines

For this dish removing the spine is not really necessary. When cooked, the bones are very easily removed during eating.

INGREDIENTS:

>   1 *kg large anchovies*
>   50 *g chopped parsley*
>   3 *teaspoons oregano*
>   3 *cloves chopped garlic*
>   *olive oil*
>   *bread crumbs*
>   *juice of 3 lemons*
>   *freshly ground pepper*
>   *salt*

Clean and gut the fish, and remove the backbone if desired. Wash in running cold water then arrange the clean fish in a colander and let it drain.

Cover the bottom of an ovenproof, shallow casserole with oil and sprinkle with bread crumbs.

Close the fish by folding it and arrange it in the casserole forming one layer, sprinkle first with salt and pepper, then with the mixture of chopped garlic and parsley and finally with a little oregano.

Cover again with bread crumbs and repeat with another layer until you have used all the fish, finishing with the herbs and bread crumbs.

Bake for about 30 minutes.

Serves 4-6

Fried Anchovies or Sardines

The recipe calls for the fish to be dipped in eggs before frying. However, coating the fish in flour only is, in my opinion, much tastier.

For a change the fish can be dipped in flour, egg and bread crumbs and served with wedges of lemon, but of course, that is another dish.

INGREDIENTS:

> *600 g fresh anchovies or sardines*
> *3 tablespoons chopped parsley*
> *2 lightly beaten eggs*
> *4 finely chopped cloves garlic*
> *some plain flour*
> *olive oil*
> *freshly ground pepper*
> *salt*

With a fine, pointed knife cut off the head then put the point of the knife into the tiny hole near the tail and cut the fish open. Remove the entrails. Wash under running cold water then arrange the clean fish in a colander and let it drain.

Open the fish, remove the spine and flatten the fish. Coat each fish with flour, then dip it into the eggs and cover again with flour.

Heat the oil in a heavy frying pan and fry the fish until golden brown.

When all the fish is fried, discard excess oil, leaving in the frying pan only enough oil to stir fry the garlic and parsley until the garlic is lightly browned, then pour it over the fish and serve immediately.

For a change, after dipping the fish in the egg, it can be coated with bread crumbs, fried, and served with wedges of lemon.

Serves 6

Anchovies or Sardines with Artichokes

This is originally a Roman recipe, but it is very popular in all of Southern Italy, when artichokes are in season. That is no problem in Napoli where artichokes, sardines and anchovies are in season at the same time.

INGREDIENTS:

> 800 *g sardines*
>   6 *tablespoons chopped parsley*
>   3 *tablespoons bread crumbs*
>   7 *artichokes*
>   *juice of half a large lemon*
>   *freshly ground pepper*
>   *salt*

With a fine, pointed knife cut off the head then put the point of the knife into the tiny hole near the tail and cut the fish open. Remove the entrails. Open each fish and remove the spine, as well as the small dorsal fin. Wash in running cold water then arrange the clean fish in a colander and let it drain.

Leave about 3–4 cm of the stems attached to the artichokes, remove the outer leaves and the outer layer of the stem, cut off the top of the leaves, so that you have only the tender part, the heart of the artichoke left, then cut the artichokes lengthways into thin slices.

Preheat oven to 350°F or 180°C. Oil an ovenproof serving dish approximately 25 cm in diameter and arrange the artichoke slices into a single layer on the bottom of the dish. Sprinkle with salt, pepper, parsley and oil, then put a layer of sardines over the artichokes, arranging the fish in a circle with the tails converging in the middle of the dish.

Sprinkle with salt, pepper, parsley and oil, then repeat with another layer of artichokes and finish with a layer of sardines, sprinkled again with salt, pepper, parsley, oil, a generous handful of bread crumbs, and another sprinkling of oil over the bread crumbs.

Bake for 45 minutes.

When you are ready to serve, sprinkle the lemon juice over the top of the dish.

Serves 6

Stuffed Anchovies or Sardines

The rolled fish looks very attractive and is often used for buffet meals. Like any other recipe for anchovies, this one, too, can be prepared with sardines.

INGREDIENTS:

>   *1 kg fresh anchovies*
>   *olive oil*
>
>   *Stuffing:*
> *100 g chopped pitted black olives*
> *50 g chopped capers*
> *50 g chopped tinned anchovy fillets*
> *1–3 tablespoons bread crumbs*

With a fine, pointed knife cut off the head then put the point of the knife into the tiny hole near the tail, cut the fish open and remove the entrails. Open each fish and remove the spine, as well as the small dorsal fin. Wash in running cold water then arrange the clean fish in a colander and let it drain.

Preheat the oven to 350°F or 180°C.

Put the tinned anchovy fillets, olives and capers, into a bowl, add part of the bread crumbs, and mix until smooth.

Arrange the fish, open side up, and put a little of the stuffing across the wide part of each fish, roll the fish towards the tail. Put each little roll into an ovenproof serving dish, so that the tail remains under the rolled fish, and the rolls form only one layer.

Sprinkle with the remaining bread crumbs and, if you have a surplus of the stuffing, sprinkle that over the fish, as well as a little olive oil.

Bake for 30 minutes.

Serves 6

Sardines in 'Saor'

A very old Venetian recipe given to me by a friend in whose family the recipe was passed on for generations. I found the same recipe very popular in Dalmatia where the Venetian Doges reigned centuries ago.

Editor's note: The recipe may well predate the Doges. The sweet-sour flavours were common in ancient Roman cookery. Saor is probably the Venetian dialect word for savour or relish.

INGREDIENTS:

> 1 *kg large fresh sardines*
> 1 *kg finely sliced onion*
> 1½ *cups vinegar*
>   *pine nuts, optional*
>   *seedless raisins, optional*
>   *finely cut lime or lemon peel*
>   *plain flour*
>   *freshly ground pepper*
>   *salt*

Clean the fish as usual, but you need to remove the spines if you want to save time.

Pat the fish dry with a paper towel, cover it with flour and deep fry.

In a saucepan heat the oil and, on a very low flame, slowly fry the sliced onion until it is transparent but not coloured, add the vinegar, continue to boil briskly until the onion is very soft.

While the onion is boiling add the optional ingredients, if you like them (I add only the pine nuts), stir for 5 minutes and remove from the stove.

In a container that can be kept in the fridge and has a well-fitting lid, arrange the fish and the onion in alternate layers, then pour in enough liquid to cover the fish completely, and refrigerate.

Serve after 2–3 days, at room temperature.

Editor's note: You may wish to add some olive oil just before serving.

Stuffed Sardines

This is one of my favourite fish dishes, even though the fresh sardine is considered the fish of the poor because it is cheap, and because you have to clean it yourself.

I admit that I am very biased regarding the humble sardine. Sardines and mackerel were the only source of protein we had during the war when my mother and I spent nearly three years in a village on an island in Dalmatia.

The main source of food was the sea. The small quantity of fish that were being caught by the few fishermen still left in the village during the brief summer season were mostly sardines. Each catch was rationed between the cannery that worked for the army, the locals and the refugees. Needless to say each ration was greatly treasured. The sardines were counted, one third—usually two or three sardines—were cooked and eaten fresh. The rest were cleaned and packed in coarse salt with lots of sliced onion, for the winter.

INGREDIENTS:

> 30 *large fresh sardines*
> *olive oil*
>
> *Stuffing:*
> 12 *chopped tinned anchovy fillets*
> 30 *g fresh bread crumbs*
> 1 *egg*
> 1 *egg yolk*

With a fine, pointed knife cut off the head then put the point of the knife into the tiny hole near the tail, cut the fish open and remove the entrails. Open each fish and remove the spine, as well as the small dorsal fin. Wash in running cold water then arrange the clean fish in a colander and let it drain.

Soak the bread in water and squeeze dry, chop the anchovy fillets very finely and, together with the soaked bread and egg yolk, mash until smooth. There are two options for stuffing the fish:

a. with a knife spread some stuffing along one half of the fish, fold the fish over, cover it with flour, dip it into the beaten eggs then cover with bread crumbs and fry; or

b. spread the stuffing over a whole open fish, cover it with another fish, press firmly together then dip into flour, eggs and bread crumbs, and deep fry.

I prefer option 'a' because I found that with option 'b' the two fish often separated and the stuffing falls out.

Whichever way you choose to do it, serve it piping hot and garnished with wedges of lemon and sprigs of parsley.

Fish Fillets with Olives

This dish is delicious when served cold and is often served on the Sabbath.

INGREDIENTS:

    8 fish fillets of your choice
  100 g pitted green olives cut into halves
    juice of 4 lemons
    olive oil
    chopped parsley
    freshly ground pepper
    salt

Place the fillets of fish into a shallow dish with the lemon juice and allow to marinate for a couple of hours. If the lemon juice does not cover the fish, turn the fish a few times whilst marinating.

Preheat the oven to 350°F or 180°C.

Take the fish fillets out of the marinade and put them in an ovenproof serving dish, forming one layer. Sprinkle with a little of the marinade, oil, salt and pepper.

Bake for 15 minutes.

Take the dish out of the oven, sprinkle the olives and parsley over the fish and return to the oven for another 5 minutes.

Serves 4

Tuna with Peas

When I was a little girl I remember holidaying with my parents in Kotar. Kotar is situated in a lovely bay on the southern end of the Yugoslav Adriatic Coast in Crna Gora (Monte Negro). It was there that I first saw the 'tonara'.

Tonare were very narrow ladders that rose high from the edge of the coast, and lent precariously forward far out over the sea. On the very top of the ladder perched a man, who, during the tuna fishing season, kept watch day and night.

When he spotted a shoal of tuna swimming towards the entrance of the bay, he shouted and waved a red flag. As soon as this signal was seen the fishermen would raise the net that was strung across the narrow opening of the bay, and the tuna had no choice but to swim into the net and be caught.

I wonder if this method is still used, or if radar replaced it. The last time I saw a tonara was in 1975.

INGREDIENTS:

> 500 g tuna
>   1 kg shelled peas
> 200 g peeled tomatoes
>   or
>   1 tablespoon concentrated tomato paste
>   1 cup chopped parsley
>   2 largish chopped onions
>   3 finely chopped cloves garlic
>   ¾ cup olive oil
>   freshly ground pepper
>   salt

Have the fishmonger cut the tuna crosswise into 3-centimetre-thick slices.

In a wide saucepan heat the oil, add the onion and when the onion begins to take on colour, add the garlic and parsley, and stir fry on a medium heat until both are lightly browned.

If you like spicy food add a little chilli to the sauce before you add the fish. Coat the tuna slices with flour, increase the heat and place the slices of tuna on top of the fried mixture. Sprinkle with salt and pepper, and fry the tuna slices on both sides, turning them carefully.

When the fish is lightly browned, add the peeled tomatoes or the tomato paste, diluted with a little water, and continue to simmer for about 15–20 minutes.

When the fish is ready remove it, leaving all the sauce in the saucepan. Arrange the fish on an warm, ovenproof serving dish, cover and keep hot in the oven, but do not bake.

Bring the sauce to the boil, add the peas and cook covered, stirring occasionally on a low heat, until the peas are tender.

When you are ready to serve, pour the hot sauce over the fish.

Serves 4

Moses' Red Mullet

My little nephew explained to me that I must not call this dish 'Fish in Tomato Sauce', because the tomato sauce is really the red sea. Call it as you will, it is a delicious dish and, of course other fish can be used.

INGREDIENTS:

> 1 kg red mullet
> 350 g seeded peeled tomatoes
> 6 tablespoons olive oil
> 3 tablespoons chopped parsley
> 3 teaspoons basil
> 2 cloves finely chopped garlic
> freshly ground pepper
> salt

Heat the oil in a wide, shallow saucepan, add the parsley and garlic, and just before the garlic begins to take on colour, pour in the tomatoes.

Stirring frequently, allow the tomato sauce to simmer until it thickens, then arrange the fish in the saucepan forming one layer only, season with salt and pepper, sprinkle with basil, and continue to cook for about 15 minutes. Shake the saucepan frequently so that the fish does not stick to the bottom, and spoon the sauce over the fish to ensure that the fish cooks thoroughly, without having to turn it.

Serves 4

Sand Mullet Baked with Vinegar

This is one of my family's favourite fish dishes. I have tried it with various other fish but none tastes as good as the mullet.

INGREDIENTS:

> 1 kg whole sand mullet
> 1 cup finely chopped parsley
> ½ cup finely chopped garlic
> 1 cup vinegar
> 1 cup olive oil
> freshly ground pepper
> salt

Preheat the oven to 350°F or 180°C.

At a distance of about 4 centimetres from each other, make crosswise incisions in the fish, cutting to the bone but not through the bone. The cuts should run from the dorsal fin to the belly. Turn the fish over and cut corresponding slits on the other side.

Pour a little of the oil and vinegar into a baking dish and put in the fish. Mix the parsley with the garlic, salt and pepper. Hold the cuts in the fish open and fill each cut with as much of the mixture as you can get into it. Turn the fish and repeat. Put part of the remaining mixture inside the fish cavity, and the remainder around it, then pour the remaining oil and vinegar over the fish.

Turning the fish over whilst it bakes is not necessary but it is very important to baste it generously and frequently. Thirty to 40 minutes should be sufficient baking time.

Baked Red Mullet

My friend Marco, who contributed this recipe to my collection, assured me that this dish is traditionally served in Rome for dinner to break the fast after Yom Kippur.

INGREDIENTS:

> 1.5 *kg whole red mullets*
> 150 *g pine nuts*
> 300 *g sultanas*
> 1 *cup olive oil*
> 1½ *cups vinegar*
> *freshly ground pepper*
> *salt*

Preheat the oven to 350°F or 180°C.

Arrange the fish in a baking dish, pour the oil and vinegar over the fish, sprinkle with salt, sultanas and pine nuts, cover and bring to the boil on a medium flame, boil slowly for 15 minutes.

Uncover, put it into the oven and bake, basting frequently, for about 30 minutes or until the fish has absorbed most of the vinegar and has become a golden colour.

Serves 8

Marinated Flounder

Zia Ulda explained to me that this is a very old Venetian way of marinating fish. It is a very delicate, piquant marinade, not indicated for long preservation of the fish. However, it is well suited for buffet dinners or luncheons. It is also a practical summer dish as it must be prepared one day in advance.

Editor's note: This is really a soglia in saor, *a traditional Venetian dish which is often made with sardines instead of the more expensive flounder or sole. It also uses the sweet-sour flavours of vinegar and sultanas, and may even date back to ancient Roman times. The common use of sweet and sour flavours in many Italian fish recipes suggests they are very old recipes indeed.*

INGREDIENTS:

> 1 *kg flounder*
> 50 *g sultanas*
> 50 *g pine nuts*
> 4 *tablespoons vinegar*
> ½ *glass white wine*
> 4 *thinly sliced onions*
> *plain flour*
> *olive oil*
> *freshly ground pepper*
> *salt*

Have the fishmonger clean the flounder and remove the heads.

Cover the fish with flour, then shake off the excess flour and fry in hot oil, turning it very carefully so as not to break it.

Remove the fish from the frying pan with a slotted spatula to eliminate as much oil as possible, and arrange it on a serving dish. If you have more than one fish arrange it in one layer only.

Sieve the oil in which you have fried the fish, put the oil in a saucepan and heat, add the sliced onion and as soon as the onion takes on colour, add the vinegar, wine, sultanas, pine nuts, salt and pepper, and let it simmer slowly for about 20 minutes.

After 20 minutes pour the hot sauce over the fish. As the fish must be covered by the sauce arrange it in a serving dish so that you will not have to turn it. Cover the dish and let it stand until cold, then refrigerate for at least 24 hours before serving.

Flounder in Wine

This is a truly delicious dish but it takes a bit of juggling to get the
timing right. To make things easier, I usually prepare everything in
advance; that is, before I join the family and friends at the table for
the first course, I cook the fish and the sauce, up to the point where
I remove the sauce from the fire to let it cool, then, after removing
the dishes of the first course, I finish the sauce and serve the fish.

It does not matter if a little time is allowed to pass between courses,
on the contrary, whatever type of food is served, it is enjoyed much
more when it is served at a leisurely pace than if the dishes are whisked
away as soon as the last morsel is put in the mouth and the next course
is served before that last morsel is swallowed.

There is an old and rather lovely saying in Italian: 'A tavola non si
invecchia!' It means: 'One does not grow older around the dining table.'

INGREDIENTS:

     4 *flounders*
  100 *g butter*
     3 *tablespoons olive oil*
     1 *tablespoon butter*
     1 *tablespoon milk or cream*
     1 *cup dry white wine*
     1 *egg yolk*
      freshly ground pepper
      salt

Preheat the oven to 350°F or 180°C.

Arrange the fish in an oiled baking dish in one layer, sprinkle with
oil, salt and pepper and pour the wine over the fish. Basting frequently,
bake for about 10–15 minutes, or till the fish is cooked.

When the fish is ready, carefully, without breaking it, remove it from
the baking dish, and place it on a serving dish, again forming only one
layer. Cover and keep hot.

Pour all the pan juices from the baking dish through a fine sieve
into a small saucepan and boil briskly until reduced to nearly half the
quantity. Remove from the heat and allow to cool.

Dilute the egg yolk with either the milk or the cream and stir it into
the sauce.

Return the saucepan to a low heat and, stirring constantly with a wooden spoon, cook slowly until the sauce thickens, then continuing to stir, remove it from the heat, add the butter, and as soon as the butter has melted and blended into the sauce, pour the sauce over the fish and serve.

Serves 4

Tossed Boiled Stockfish

Stockfish (Baccala), is a cold water fish caught off the shores of Norway and sold in Italy salt dried, so that it must always be soaked at least overnight before it is cooked. It is very popular in southern Italy where it is considered the fish of the poor even though it is often served in many households that are far from being poor because it is very tasty. Locally it is readily available in many Italian groceries and supermarkets.

This is one of my favourite fish dishes. It is a very simple dish to prepare—you really do not need to use the cheese cloth.

INGREDIENTS:

> 700 g stockfish
>   4 tablespoons olive oil
>   2 tablespoons chopped parsley
>   2 cloves garlic, squeezed
>   freshly ground pepper
>   salt

Soak the fish in cold water for 24 hours or at least overnight, changing the water several times.

Wrap the fish in muslin or cheese cloth and put it into a saucepan. Cover the fish with water, add a pinch of salt and bring it to the boil.

When the fish had boiled for 10 minutes, take it out of the water, put it on a plate and check for any remaining bones or skin, which should be removed.

Put the fish, breaking it up but not cutting it, into a bowl, add the oil, garlic and parsley, cover the bowl with a plate that is slightly larger than the bowl itself then, gripping it firmly with both hands, hold the bowl and plate together and shake it energetically up and down for as long as you can.

The longer the fish is tossed, the tastier it becomes.

Serve cold with a fresh side salad.

Serves 5

Baked Stockfish with Spinach

This recipe comes from Venice, where I was told that it is also known as the Jewish Fish.

INGREDIENTS:
> *500 g stockfish*
> *1.5 kg fresh spinach*
> *2 tablespoons butter*
> *2 tablespoons grated Gruyère cheese*
> *1 cup besciamelle sauce (see recipe page 214)*
> *pinch of grated nutmeg*
> *½ cup bread crumbs*
> *freshly ground pepper*
> *salt*

Soak the fish in cold water for 24 hours or at least overnight, changing the water several times.

Prepare an ovenproof, serving pie dish by rubbing it with butter and sprinkling it with bread crumbs.

Wash the fish thoroughly, boil it until tender, remove all traces of skin and bones and chop it, not too finely, either by hand or in the food processor.

Steam or boil the spinach until al dente, drain and rinse under cold water, then squeeze dry and chop coarsely.

Heat one and a half tablespoons of butter in a saucepan, add the chopped spinach and cook it in the butter for a few minutes, stirring it well, so that it absorbs the flavour of the butter.

Remove the saucepan from the heat, add the besciamelle sauce, the nutmeg and the fish, and mix it all with a wide wooden spoon until it is well amalgamated.

Preheat the oven to 350°F or 180°C.

Place the mixture into the prepared pie dish, sprinkle it with the grated cheese, dot it with a few nuts of butter, and bake for 30 to 40 minutes.

Serves 4

Venetian Baked Stockfish

Stockfish is a very popular dish in Venice. The Venetians say that stockfish and polenta make a perfect team.

INGREDIENTS:

> 1 *kg stockfish*
> 4 *tablespoons plain flour*
> 4 *tablespoons grated Parmesan*
> 2 *tablespoons chopped parsley*
> 4 *tablespoons butter*
> 1 *teaspoon nutmeg*
> 3 *cups milk*
> 1 *cup white wine*
> 1 *cup olive oil*
> 1 *small chopped onion*
> 1 *clove crushed garlic*
> 8 *anchovy fillets*
> *freshly ground pepper*
> *salt*

Soak the fish in cold water for 24 hours or at least overnight, changing the water several times.

Cut the fish into chunks or slices, arrange the slices in one layer in an ovenproof serving dish that has a well fitting lid, sprinkle the fish with salt, pepper, nutmeg and Parmesan.

In a saucepan heat the oil, add the onion and garlic and fry. As soon as the onion begins to brown add the anchovies and stir fry until the anchovies disintegrate. Add the wine and the parsley, and simmer slowly until all the wine evaporates.

When the wine has evaporated add the milk and butter, stir well and pour over the fish pieces. Cover the dish, place it into the oven and bake at low heat for at least two hours, or until the fish has absorbed the milk.

Serve hot with polenta.

Serves 6

Stockfish Cutlets

Left over stockfish cutlets are delicious served cold with a side salad.

INGREDIENTS:
> *500 g stockfish*
> *50 g melted butter*
> *1 tablespoon grated cheese*
> *4 anchovy fillets*
> *6 sprigs parsley*
> *2 eggs, lightly beaten*
> *3 slices stale white bread*
> *bread crumbs*
> *freshly ground pepper*
> *salt*

Put the stockfish through the mincer together with the anchovies and the parsley. Soak the bread in water, squeeze dry, and place it into a mixing bowl together with the fish. Add the melted butter, cheese and pepper, and check for salt.

Knead well to amalgamate all ingredients. You can do that with a wide wooden spoon, but I find it much easier to knead it by hand.

Form round patties, one at a time. Put the patty on the bread crumbs and flatten it with the palm of your hand. The shape of the patty should be similar to a cutlet. Turn it over so that both sides are well covered with bread crumbs. Dip the cutlet into the beaten eggs and again cover it well with bread crumbs on both sides. Fry until the cutlets are golden brown and crisp.

Serves 6

Stewed Mullet

I do not really know whether this is a typically Jewish recipe or not, because it is so widely used in Italy. The recipe I was given by my friend Virginia calls for mullet, but there is no reason why any other firmly fleshed fish should not be used.

INGREDIENTS:

> *sand mullets, whole, of approx. 300–400 g each*
> *for each mullet you will need:*
> 1 *teaspoon tomato paste*
> 1 *finely chopped celery stalk*
> 2 *anchovy fillets*
> *lemon juice*
> *olive oil*
> *freshly ground pepper*
> *salt (careful with the salt, anchovies are salty)*

Put the chopped celery into a saucepan (according to the old recipe the saucepan should be of copper), with a little oil and stir fry until golden. Add the anchovy fillets and stir with a wooden spoon until the anchovies disintegrate, then add the fish, and allow it to fry for a few minutes on each side, turning the fish very carefully without breaking it.

Dilute the tomato paste with a little water, and add it to the fish. Season with salt and pepper, and add enough water to cover half the fish, cover the saucepan and simmer slowly, turning the fish once when half cooked.

Add the lemon juice and cook for another 3 or 4 minutes, remove the fish from the sauce, place it on a heated serving dish and keep warm.

If the sauce is too liquid, continue to boil briskly until reduced, then pour the sauce over the fish, and serve.

Flounder Maitre d'

It is well worth while to take the time and trouble necessary to prepare this dish, it really is a masterpiece of taste, as well as presentation. It does not sound like a traditional Jewish dish but I have seen it served at Bar Mitzvahs and weddings in Italy.

INGREDIENTS:

>   *500 g flounder*
>   *100 g butter*
>   *½ cup full cream*
>   *¼ cup white dry marsala*
>   *2 medium finely grated carrots*
>   *8 heads of medium-sized mushrooms*
>   *4 medium-sized tomatoes cut into halves*
>   *1 finely chopped truffle*
>   *finely chopped parsley for garnishing*
>   *olive oil*
>   *freshly ground pepper*
>   *salt*

>   *Besciamelle:*
>   *30 g plain flour*
>   *30 g butter*
>   *¼ litre milk*
>   *pinch of grated nutmeg*
>   *freshly ground pepper*
>   *salt*

Heat the butter in a small saucepan and as soon as it is melted add the grated carrots and the chopped truffle, sprinkle it with a little salt, cover and simmer.

Place the flounder in a baking dish. If you have more than one fish arrange the fish next to each other forming only one layer.

Preheat the oven to 350°F or 180°C.

When the carrots are tender add the marsala, stir and allow it to heat on the fire for about 2 minutes, but be careful not to let it boil. Pour the contents of the saucepan over the fish and bake for 20 minutes, basting frequently.

In a small baking dish place the tomato halves, sprinkle with oil, salt and pepper and simmer for 10 minutes, and set aside.

In another saucepan sauté the mushroom heads in the remaining butter until cooked, and set aside.

Prepare the besciamelle sauce (see page 214) with the quantity of ingredients given above.

When the fish is cooked, transfer it carefully, without breaking it, on to a preheated serving dish and keep warm.

Pour the besciamelle sauce and the cream into the baking dish with the fish juices, place the baking dish on the heat just long enough to stir well, amalgamate all the ingredients and heat the sauce without allowing it to boil, then pour the sauce over the fish.

Place the cooked tomato halves, cut side up, on the serving dish, either four each side of the fish or all around the fish depending on the shape of the dish, then place a mushroom head on each tomato, round side up, sprinkle everything with the chopped parsley and serve piping hot.

Flounder in Aspic

Because of the flounder's delicate flavour, this was Nonna Rina's favourite recipe for fish in aspic. When Nonna Rina was ill and had no appetite, this was one of the few dishes I could coax her to eat.

I used to put on Nonna Rina's plate a small flounder which I had decorated with a smiling face. It was a foolproof way of making Nonna smile and eat her dinner.

Make the eyes with two halves of a black olive, cut a thin round slice of a green pepper and from that cut out two eyebrows; from a slice of red pepper or from a tomato slice cut the mouth and arrange it so that it turns upwards into a smile; make the nostrils with two peppercorns, and there you have it—a smiling fish!

INGREDIENTS:

    1 kg flounder whole
    3 tablespoons olive oil
    juice of 1 lemon
    pinch of saffron, optional
    freshly ground pepper
    salt

Place the flounders in a wide shallow dish with just enough water to cover the fish, add the oil, salt and pepper and simmer very slowly for 10 to 15 minutes, or until the eyes are clouded.

When the fish has cooled, with a broad spatula lift off the top half of the fish and place it on a serving dish, then, slowly and carefully lift off the backbone and the head, discard these, lift the bottom half of the fish and place it on the serving dish.

Continue this operation until all the fish are boned and arranged on the serving dish.

Add the lemon juice and saffron to the pan juices and simmer until the juices are reduced so that you have only enough left to barely cover the fish.

When refrigerated, the sauce becomes jelly, and served garnished with parsley and lemon slices, it looks lovely and tastes delicious.

It is obviously a popular dish for Sabbath, as it can be prepared well in advance.

Serves 6

Blue Freshwater Fish

For this method of cooking fish, only sweet (fresh) water fish should be used, hence it is a popular recipe in the inland regions of Italy, and not along the coast where sea fish is prevalent.

INGREDIENTS:

> 1　*white freshwater fish of your choice*
> *vinegar*
>
> *Stock:*
> *onion*
> *celery stalk*
> *carrot*
> *parsley*
> *bay leaf*
> *vary the quantities according to the size of the fish*
> *freshly ground pepper*
> *salt*

Lift the perforated tray out of the fish kettle and place the whole fish on the tray, set aside.

Place all the vegetables in the fish kettle with enough water to cover the fish and boil for about 30 minutes.

Put the vinegar into a small saucepan, and bring it to the boil. Hook the tray with the fish onto the sides of the kettle, pour the boiling vinegar over the whole fish, and immediately immerse the fish in the boiling broth, having first raised the flame to prevent the soup from ceasing to boil when the fish is added to it. Cover the kettle, lower the heat and continue to simmer until the fish is cooked.

Transfer the whole fish to a heated serving plate and serve piping hot, with boiled potatoes sprinkled with chopped parsley.

Fish Stew

I believe that this is not an original Italian dish but, as I have been served this dish at various festive occasions in Italian Jewish homes, I have included it.

INGREDIENTS:

> 2 *kg assorted fish: red mullet, sole, sea bream, hake and grey mullet*
> 2 *tablespoons tomato paste*
> 1 *cup finely chopped parsley*
> 1 *large onion finely sliced*
> 1 *French bread stick sliced and oven toasted*
> ½ *cup olive oil*
> ¾ *cup vinegar*
> *freshly ground pepper*
> *salt*

Use a wide saucepan as the fish should be placed flat next to each other, forming only one layer, without overlapping.

Heat the oil, and when it is hot add the finely sliced onion, season with salt and pepper and stir fry until the onion begins to colour. Add the parsley and continue to stir fry for another few minutes before adding the tomato paste diluted with a little water.

Stir, and allow to simmer until the ingredients are well blended, then add the vinegar. Cover the saucepan, lower the heat and continue to boil very slowly for about one hour, or until the onion has disintegrated completely. Stir frequently and, if needed, add a little water from time to time, keeping in mind that you will need enough sauce to cover the toasted bread.

Add the fish, first the larger fish, and about 8–10 minutes later, the smaller fish, cover the saucepan and cook over a very low heat for 30 minutes. Check frequently and, if needed, add a little water so the sauce is not reduced too much.

To serve: either arrange the toast on a heated serving dish, forming one layer, cover the bread slices with the sauce, then place the fish on top and garnish with sprigs of parsley; or serve only the fish on a heated serving dish and the sauce in a well heated sauce boat, with the crisp slices of hot toast in a bread basket.

Serves 6

Fried Fish Slices

Decorated with black olives, this makes a very nice-looking and different fish dish for festive occasions. Although it can be prepared with any fish, the result is best when white fish such as snapper is used. It is meant to be a cold dish but is also very nice when freshly cooked and served hot.

INGREDIENTS:

> 1 *kg fish slices of your choice*
> 1 *cup chopped parsley*
> 1 *glass water*
> 1 *crushed clove garlic*
> *juice of 3 lemons*
> *olive oil*
> *freshly ground pepper*
> *salt*

Have the fishmonger slice the fish crosswise to form slices 2–3 centimetres thick.

Heat the oil in a large frying pan, add the garlic then the fish slices, placing the slices next to each other to form one layer only, then add the water, lemon juice, salt, pepper and parsley.

Cook slowly for 20–30 minutes, transfer to a serving dish and allow to cool in its own sauce which, when cold, will form a jelly.

Serve cold with boiled potatoes or potato salad.

Serves 6

Tuna Loaf

A lovely summer dish for luncheons or buffet dinners, it is also practical for picnics as it can be easily packed as a roll then sliced and covered with mayonnaise when ready to serve.

INGREDIENTS:

> 200 g tin of tuna in oil
> 100 g bread crumbs
> 50 g grated cheese, optional
> 2 eggs
> pinch of grated nutmeg
> freshly ground pepper
> salt

Mince the tuna very finely, or mash it in the food processor, add the eggs, bread crumbs and nutmeg and mix until smooth.

Take the mixture out of the mixing bowl, put it on the working surface and shape into the form of a salami, but be careful that you do not make the salami too long as it has to fit into the saucepan.

Roll the tuna salami firmly into a cheese cloth or alfoil and put it into a saucepan with just enough boiling water to cover the roll. Boil for 30 minutes, allowing a large part of the water to evaporate.

After 30 minutes, carefully, take the roll out of the saucepan, do not break it, let it cool completely and refrigerate it for a few hours.

Cut the roll into slices about 2cm thick, arrange on a serving dish and serve either garnished with sprigs of parsley and slices of lemon, covered with mayonnaise, or with salsa verde.

Serves 3-4

Tuna Croquettes

This is the Italian version of the universal Jewish staple: the salmon patty! It makes a nice change.

INGREDIENTS:

> *100 g tinned tuna in oil*
> *2 tablespoons grated Parmesan cheese*
> *1 cup besciamelle sauce (see page 214)*
> *½ cup water*
> *½ cup milk*
> *1 egg, separated*
> *olive oil*
> *freshly ground pepper*
> *salt*

Put the tuna into a bowl without breaking it up, cover it with the watered milk, and let it stand for 2 hours.

Prepare the besciamelle with a little less milk than the recipe indicates, as you need a fairly thick besciamelle for the croquettes.

Strain the tuna, put it into a mixing bowl and crumble it with a fork until it is completely disintegrated. Add the besciamelle, cheese, egg yolk, salt and pepper to taste, and with a wooden spoon mix all the ingredients together until smooth.

Beat the egg white till stiff.

Take a spoonful of the mixture at a time, form little balls, keeping your hands wet with cold water. Coat each ball with the beaten egg white and fry, a few at a time, in hot oil.

If, when you start to form the balls, you find that the mixture is too soft, add some bread crumbs.

Place the fried croquettes on a couple of layers of paper towels to drain. Serve hot or cold.

Zia Lea's Tuna Mousse

This is the original recipe as it was given to me by my sister-in-law. However, I found that by putting all the ingredients into a blender at the same time, the whole thing is done in a few minutes, and the result is even better.

INGREDIENTS:

100 *g tinned tuna in oil*
100 *g butter*
  2 *eggs*
     freshly ground pepper
     salt

Put the tuna into the food processor and mash until smooth. Transfer the mashed tuna into a mixing bowl, add the butter, which should be at room temperature, salt and pepper, and beat with a wooden spoon, or put it into the blender and work until frothy.

Add the eggs, one at a time, beating each egg well into the mixture before adding the next one.

Rinse a mousse form with cold water, place the mixture into the form and refrigerate for several hours.

To unmould the mousse, turn the mould upside down on to a serving plate, dip a kitchen towel into hot water, squeeze it dry and put it over the mould for a few moments only, the mould should now lift off easily.

I also add finely chopped chives and a few drops of lemon juice to the mixture.

I like to serve it garnished with alternating tomato and cucumber slices all around it, this adds colour to an otherwise rather drab looking dish.

Meat and Poultry

Meat and poultry are always served separately with only a garnish such as lemon wedges and a sprig of parsley. The only exception I remember is an occasional meat or poultry roast served with a baked potato or tiny new potatoes boiled and sprinkled with chopped parsley. A festive meal is served in the following order:

Antipasto
Pasta or Soup
Fish
Poultry
Meat
Vegetables
Salad
Dessert
Fresh Fruit
Espresso Coffee

If two or more fish courses are served instead of poultry and meat a selection of cheeses is served with the fruit.

Of course, an everyday meal in an average family does not consist of so many courses but, whatever the number of courses served, the order in which they are served does not vary.

Rice, or in Northern Italy, polenta, is also served as a first course, not as an accompaniment for meat. Often a green vegetable is served as a first course—spinach, broccoli, silverbeet or other green, leafy vegetables. These are mostly served parboiled in salted water and dressed with olive oil and chopped garlic. Lemon juice is either used in the dressing or served separately. Serving a vegetable as a first course does not preclude serving other vegetables later in the meal.

Editor's note: Italian cooking generally is rich in its use of vegetables, and Italian-Jewish cooking is even more striking in the ways in which vegetables are used. Many of the following recipes show what is thought to be the distinctively Italian-Jewish habit of combining meat and vegetables in the same dish. The custom may well derive from the demands of domestic economy and the difficulty of obtaining kosher meat; a small quantity of meat can be 'stretched' to feed more people if vegetables are added to it.

Veal Cutlets with Lettuce

This is a very old Roman recipe, still very popular. Nonna Rina often asked for it to be prepared when she had an upset stomach. Cooked lettuce is believed to be soothing and beneficial for digestion. It is also a good natural diuretic.

Editor's note: As far back as Apicius, the ancient Roman gourmet and cookery writer who lived during the time of Tiberius, lettuce was believed to be beneficial for the digestion.

INGREDIENTS:

> 8 *thin slices of veal*
> 1 *head of lettuce*
> *plain flour*
> *olive oil*
> *freshly ground pepper*
> *salt*

Lay each slice of veal flat on the chopping board and beat it with a meat mallet until the meat is of an even thickness all over.

Heat the oil in a frying pan. Dust the veal slices with flour and fry them in the hot oil till they are golden brown on both sides.

Preheat the oven to 350°F or 180°C.

Arrange four slices flat on the bottom of an ovenproof dish, cover with three layers of lettuce leaves, put the remaining four slices of veal over the lettuce leaves and cover with three more layers of lettuce.

Sprinkle with a little of the oil that you used for frying the meat, and bake for 30 minutes.

Serves 4

Veal and Onion Rolls

INGREDIENTS:

>   700 g thin veal slices
>   500 g sliced mushrooms
>   5 tablespoons olive oil
>   1 tablespoon chopped parsley
>   1 teaspoon dry oregano
>   2 sliced onions
>   2 chopped onions
>   2 cloves crushed garlic
>   beef stock
>   freshly ground pepper
>   salt
>   toothpicks

Heat a little oil in a saucepan, add half of the chopped onion and fry till the onion becomes transparent. Add the garlic and continue to fry until the onion and garlic are lightly browned, then add the mushrooms and simmer over a low heat for 15 minutes.

When the mushrooms are ready put them into a sieve and place the sieve over a bowl to drain the oil while you cook the meat.

Lay each slice of veal flat on the chopping board and beat it with a meat mallet until it is of an even thickness all over.

Sprinkle a pinch of oregano and some freshly ground black pepper over all the meat slices, then put some of the mushroom and onion mixture on each slice of meat, roll the meat tightly over the filling and put a toothpick through the meat to keep it in place.

Put the oil and the remaining onion mixture into a shallow saucepan, wide enough to accommodate the meat rolls in one layer only.

Fry the remaining onion until it is light brown, then put it into the saucepan with the meat rolls, together with a cup of stock, and simmer slowly over a low heat. Turn the meat rolls frequently and when necessary add a little stock.

When the meat is tender, add the mushrooms and the onions from the sieve, and with a wooden spoon move the meat rolls about until the mushrooms are heated through.

To serve, place the meat on a warmed platter and pour the sauce over the rolls.

Serves 6

Veal Fricasse

Fricasse should not be reheated, not even in the microwave. When reheated, the sauce becomes a gluggy mess.

INGREDIENTS:

> 750 *g thin veal slices*
>   5 *tablespoons olive oil*
>   1 *egg*
>   *plain flour*
>   *juice of one lemon*
>   *stock*
>   *freshly ground pepper*
>   *salt*

Lay each slice of veal flat on the chopping board and beat it with a meat mallet till it is of an even thickness all over.

Cover each slice of meat with seasoned flour. Arrange the meat slices, together with the oil and a little stock, in a shallow saucepan and simmer over a low flame for about 20 minutes, adding a little stock when needed to keep the cutlets moist.

When the cutlets are tender arrange them on a preheated serving dish and keep them hot while you prepare the sauce.

Whisk the egg lightly, add the lemon juice and continue to whisk until well blended.

Return the saucepan with the pan juices to a low heat, stir with a wooden spoon, and as soon as the pan juices are hot, whilst continuing to stir, slowly pour in the egg and lemon mixture. Continue to stir until the sauce thickens, but be very careful because the sauce must thicken without reaching boiling point, or it will become an omelette. As soon as the sauce is thick pour it over the cutlets and serve immediately.

Editor's note: The egg and lemon sauce here suggests a Sephardi origin. Lemons are common in Italian cooking, since they grow so well in Italy, but no one else uses lemon so frequently with veal.

Serves 6

Veal Tongue with Olives

The tongue will be much easier to cut if you boil it in advance and cut it when it is quite cold.

INGREDIENTS:

> 1 *pickled veal tongue*
> 300 *g pitted black olives cut in thin slivers*
> 1 *tablespoon tomato paste*
> 1 *tablespoon dry basil*
> 4 *tablespoons olive oil*
> 1 *teaspoon dry oregano*
> 1 *clove garlic*
> *freshly ground pepper*

Put the tongue into a saucepan, cover with cold water and boil slowly until it is tender. Take the tongue out of the water, and remove the skin and all the fat.

When the tongue has cooled for 15 minutes slice it, cutting the slices about 3–4 mm thick.

In a smaller saucepan heat the oil, add the garlic and fry it. When it begins to colour, remove and discard it. Add the tomato paste and dilute it with a cup of water in which the tongue has boiled, add all the spices including the olives, stir well then add the sliced tongue.

The sauce should cover the sliced tongue but, if the tongue is not covered, add a little more of the water in which the tongue was boiled. Cover the saucepan and simmer for about half an hour.

Editor's note: Another recipe which seems to come from Sephardi cooking. I have seen a Balkan-Jewish version of this which uses cinnamon as well, but the flavour is an acquired taste.

Braised Veal Tongue

Braised tongue is served with small boiled new potatoes, sprinkled with chopped parsley.

INGREDIENTS:

   2 *veal tongues approx. 1kg*
 100 *g dried mushrooms*
   5 *tablespoons olive oil*
   ½ *cup dry white wine*
   4 *medium onions, chopped finely*
   1 *finely chopped carrot*
   1 *clove crushed garlic*
   1 *chopped celery stalk*
     freshly ground pepper
     salt

Soak the dried mushrooms in cold water for a couple of hours.

Put the tongue into a saucepan together with the chopped onion, carrot and celery, cover with water and bring to the boil.

Cover the saucepan, lower the heat, and boil for two hours or until the tongues are tender and the water reduced by at least half.

Take the tongues out of the water, remove the skin and all the fat, and return the tongue to the boiling water, add the oil, wine and mushrooms and continue to simmer for another half an hour uncovered to allow the sauce to thicken.

Serve the tongue covered with the sauce.

Serves 8

Veal and Eggs

INGREDIENTS:

   6 *thin slices veal of 80–90 g each*
   1 *tablespoon plain flour*
   3 *teaspoons sage*
   ½ *cup dry red wine*
   1 *cup stock*

> 6 *peeled, hard-boiled eggs*
> *olive oil*
> *freshly ground pepper*
> *salt*
> *toothpicks*

Place the veal slices flat on the working surface, sprinkle each slice with salt, pepper and a pinch of sage, then put a hard boiled egg on each slice of meat, roll the meat over the egg and put a toothpick through the meat to hold it in place.

In a wide, shallow saucepan or a deep frying pan, heat the oil and place the rolls into the hot oil, forming one layer only. Turn the rolls several times so that they brown all over, as evenly as possible.

When the meat is golden brown add the wine, cover and simmer, turning the meat rolls several times, till the wine evaporates.

Remove the rolls from the saucepan, slice them carefully, arrange on a preheated serving dish, cover and keep hot.

Mix one level teaspoon of plain flour with a cup of cold stock until there are no lumps left, then pour the mixture into the saucepan with the pan juices, stir well and boil for a few minutes until the sauce thickens.

Pour the hot sauce over the meat slices and serve immediately.

Serves 6

Aspic

Editor's note: This recipe for aspic and the recipe which follows it are also ideal for Sabbath and Festival cooking since they can be prepared ahead of time.

I have learned the following trick of the trade from my dear friend, Johnny's mother who, before the war, had a restaurant in Vienna. It works perfectly and gives the aspic a professional look.

After you have prepared the soup for the aspic and strained it through the linen towel, put the clear soup back on the fire and bring it to the boil. In the meantime beat two egg whites into a light snow, and when the soup boils, lower the heat and spread the beaten egg whites over the soup, covering the whole surface. Continue to boil very slowly for 15 minutes, then skim off the egg white, discard it and strain the soup through a clean, damp linen towel.

If, in addition to the professional clarity you also want your aspic to have a beautiful amber colour, reheat it again to boiling point, then put a little sugar into a tablespoon with a drop of water and hold it over a low heat. When the sugar has melted and is dark brown, pour a few drops, one at a time, into the boiling soup until you obtain the desired amber colour. Strain the soup through the wet linen cloth before you pour it into the mould.

INGREDIENTS:

> 500 g gravy beef
>   2 veal shanks
>   6 chicken legs
>   6 chicken necks
>   12 pepper kernels
>   salt

Put the meat into a large saucepan together with the veal shanks, chicken necks, chicken legs and two litres of water. Bring to the boil and, as soon as it starts to boil add the salt and the pepper kernels. Cover the saucepan and boil very slowly until the liquid is reduced by half. During the boiling time skim frequently until all the froth is removed.

Remove the saucepan from the heat. Strain the soup through a colander and set aside the meat which can be used for other dishes. Moisten a linen towel in cold water, squeeze it dry, place it over a bowl and sieve the soup through the wet towel. Pour the soup into a mould and refrigerate until it sets. If the aspic does not set, reheat the soup and continue to boil until it is further reduced.

To unmould the aspic, turn the mould upside down onto a serving dish, dip a kitchen towel into hot water, wring it out and put it over the mould for a few moments only, and the mould should lift off easily.

Veal in Aspic

This was Zia Lea's favourite aspic recipe. I remember being told that she received it from a friend who lived in Rome, but I am not convinced that this makes it a typically Roman recipe. However, it is an easy way to prepare a very attractive and tasteful dish suitable for any occasion.

INGREDIENTS:

> 1 *kg shoulder of veal*
> 1-2 *veal shanks*
> 1 *clove crushed garlic*
> *olive oil*
> *salt and pepper*

Sprinkle the veal with salt and pepper and tie it firmly with kitchen string to form a roll like a salami.

Heat a little oil in a saucepan, add first the garlic, then the meat. Brown the meat on a brisk heat. When the meat is browned on all sides, remove the garlic, add the veal shank, cover with water and boil slowly on a low flame until the meat is tender.

Remove the meat from the saucepan and let it cool but, if the shank is not tender at the same time as the other meat, continue to cook it until it is tender.

To clarify the broth, treat it the same way as the soup for the aspic in the previous recipe.

When the meat is cold, slice it and arrange it on a serving dish that is deep enough to allow you to pour the broth over the meat.

Refrigerate until ready to eat, and serve garnished with giardiniera (Italian mixed pickles).

Serves 8

Veal Cutlets or Chicken Rebecca

I believe that the name Rebecca was given to this dish to designate it as a typically Jewish dish. I have been served Cutlets Rebecca in different parts of Italy; the cutlets were always prepared the same way, but there was never a Rebecca in the family.

For a change, add 2-3 tablespoons of chopped mushrooms to the sauce when you add the onion, or a tablespoon of tomato paste.

INGREDIENTS:

     500 g veal slices
         or
     500 g skinned chicken breast
       4 tablespoons chopped parsley
       2 tablespoons chopped spring onion
       1 cup dry white wine
         juice of one lemon
         plain flour
         freshly ground pepper
         salt

Cover the cutlets with seasoned flour.

Heat the oil in a large frying pan, add the cutlets and fry for a few minutes on each side till golden brown. Lower the heat, add the wine and simmer until nearly all the wine has evaporated.

Arrange the cutlets on a preheated serving dish and keep hot.

Return the frying pan to the fire, add the chopped spring onion and the parsley and cook slowly for about 5 minutes, remove from the flame, add the lemon juice to the pan juices, stir and pour over the cutlets.

Serves 4

Ragù

INGREDIENTS:

     700 g diced veal
       2 cups meat stock
       ½ cup olive oil

1 *large chopped onion*
1 *clove crushed garlic*
2 *stalks celery finely chopped*
1 *small carrot grated*
1 *small tin tomato paste*
  freshly ground pepper
  salt

Heat the oil in a saucepan and when hot add the onion and garlic and sauté until lightly browned.

Add the celery and carrot and continue to stir fry for another five minutes.

Add the tomato paste and the veal and stir until well mixed. Cover the saucepan, lower the flame and continue to simmer, very slowly, until the meat is tender, adding a little hot water or stock if necessary.

The trick in preparing a good ragu is to simmer it so slowly that the meat releases its own juices, and as little extra water or stock is added as possible.

Serve with polenta or pasta.

Serves 6

Aunt Ester's Beef Ragù

I do not remember whose aunt Ester was, but she must have been a very good cook—this dish is delicious.

INGREDIENTS:

>   600 *g yearling beef, cubed*
>   350 *g shelled peas*
>   ½ *cup beef stock*
>   2 *tablespoons chopped parsley*
>   4 *chopped spring onions*
>   1 *chopped clove garlic*
>   4 *artichokes*
>   *freshly ground pepper*
>   *salt*

Clean the artichokes, discarding all the hard outer leaves and cut off the hard tops, then cut each artichoke into eight wedges. Dip into lemon juice to prevent discolouring.

Put the oil, chopped onions, garlic and parsley into a saucepan, heat and, as soon as it starts to sizzle, add the cubed meat and stir with a wooden spoon, until all the meat browns evenly.

When the meat is well sealed, add the peas, artichokes, stock, salt and pepper, cover and simmer on a low flame until the meat and vegetables are tender.

Editor's note: The combination of peas and artichokes may sound strange, but is absolutely delicious. There is a Greek vegetable stew of artichokes and peas, and the combination appears occasionally in French cooking. The use of the two vegetables with meat appears to be distinctively Italian-Jewish, and the combination of meat with artichokes is very popular in Sephardi cooking.

Serves 4

Girello Stew in Onion Sauce

Although girello is a very popular cut of meat in Italy I find that it is very often dry, whichever way it is cooked. I prefer a very young scotch fillet, or an oyster blade.

INGREDIENTS:

> *800 g yearling beef girello*
> *600 g onions sliced thin*
> *1 cup olive oil*
> *1 tablespoon plain flour*
> *freshly ground pepper*
> *salt*

In a saucepan that is wide enough to accommodate the meat, heat the oil, add the onions and fry briskly. As soon as the onion begins to sizzle, add the meat and seal it on all sides, whilst at the same time the onions should become lightly browned. Season with salt and pepper.

Mix the flour with half a cup of water until there are no lumps, pour the mixture over the onions and immediately add another cup of water. Cover the saucepan, lower the heat and continue to cook until the onions disintegrate completely.

Before removing the meat from the saucepan check if it is ready. If the meat is not yet tender, add a little water and continue to cook slowly.

When the meat is tender, remove it from the sauce and let it stand for ten minutes before you slice it. Arrange the slices on a preheated serving dish.

Stir the sauce well and pour it over the sliced meat, or pour the sauce over the whole meat and carve it at the table.

Serves 6

Lemon Beef

This recipe is also very nice if the juice and rind of an orange or a couple of limes are substituted for the lemon juice and rind.

Serve the meat with thin slices of whichever fruit was used in the cooking. Arrange the slices of fruit around the meat or in a row over the top of the meat.

INGREDIENTS:

> 600 g yearling beef, any cut that is suitable for a pot roast
> 1 cup stock
> 6 tablespoons olive oil
> juice of 1 large lemon
> grated rind of 1 lemon
> salt and pepper

Tie the meat tightly with kitchen string to make it look like a salami.

Heat the oil in a saucepan. When the oil is very hot add the meat and brown it on all sides. Lower the heat, add the lemon juice, cover the saucepan and simmer for five minutes then add the stock and continue to simmer until the meat is tender.

If necessary add more stock during the cooking time but, always a little at a time.

When ready, remove the meat from the saucepan and allow it to rest for ten minutes before slicing it.

Arrange the sliced meat on a preheated serving dish and keep hot.

Reheat the pan juices and taste for seasoning, then add the grated lemon rind, stir with a wooden spoon, bring to the boil and simmer covered for five minutes before pouring it over the sliced meat.

Serves 4

Zia Bice's Marinated Beef 1

Zia Bice, my mother-in-law's sister, gave me this recipe. One morning, when Zia Bice came to call on Nonna Rina, she broke the unwritten law and came into the kitchen.

Zia Bice, a very frugal lady, was upset when she saw what I was doing. There I was, happily pouring marinade down the drain, intending to grill the marinated meat. Such waste was unheard of in Zia Bice's household, and I was promptly given the recipe of how to use marinade.

The result of this recipe is very tasty. It is similar to the way my mother used to prepare mock venison.

INGREDIENTS:

    1 *kg prime cut of lean beef*
    2 *crushed cloves garlic*
250 *g green olives, pitted*
250 *g finely diced carrots*
    3 *stalks of finely diced celery*
    4 *medium sliced onions*
    6 *peeled tomatoes, quartered*
    3 *bay leaves*
10 *peppercorns*
    2 *tablespoons chopped parsley*
    1 *teaspoon fennel seeds*
    2 *glasses dry red wine*
    7 *tablespoons olive oil*
      stock
      salt

Heat four tablespoons of oil in a saucepan, add the onion, garlic, celery and carrot and fry slowly until light brown. Add the wine, bay leaves, peppercorns, parsley, fennel seeds and salt and continue to cook slowly on low heat for ten minutes.

Remove from the heat and allow to cool.

Put the meat into an earthenware dish just large enough to accommodate the meat and pour the marinade over the meat, cover the dish and leave in a cool place overnight.

The next day take the meat out of the marinade, and set the marinade aside. Pat the meat dry with paper towels and tie it with kitchen string so that it keeps its shape.

Heat the remaining oil in a casserole, add the meat and, turning it several times, let it brown on all sides.

When the meat is well browned add the marinade and the tomatoes, bring to boil then lower the heat, cover the casserole and simmer very slowly. If needed add a little more stock during the cooking time.

When the meat is nearly tender, add the olives and continue to simmer until the meat is ready.

Remove the meat from the casserole and allow it to rest for ten minutes before you remove the string and slice it.

Arrange the sliced meat on a preheated serving dish and keep hot.

Reheat the marinade-sauce, taste for seasoning, and if the sauce is too liquid continue to boil until it is well reduced, then pour it over the sliced meat.

Editor's note: A larger piece of meat can be used without increasing the quantities of other ingredients.

In traditional households, particularly in areas where there were no kosher butchers, most people made their own preserved meats, using some of the Italian styles of sausage making with kosher meat. There was dried beef, for instance, as well as beef and goose salami. Goose was also cured in the manner of a leg of pork, so that it was known as prosciutto. Most of the recipes are unsuitable for modern kitchens, and for people without the experience of curing meats, but the following recipes are included to show how such things were done, and the pride with which they were made.

Zia Bice's Marinated Beef 2

This is a slight variation of the previous recipe.

INGREDIENTS:

　　　 1 *kg yearling roast beef*
　　　 ½ *litre dry red wine*
　　　 ½ *cup olive oil*
　　　 3 *tablespoons chopped onion*
　　　 2 *chopped large onions*
　　　 2 *chopped medium carrots*
　　　 2 *cloves crushed garlic*
　　　 2 *stalks chopped celery*
　　　 4 *bay leaves*
　　　　 pinch grated nutmeg
　　 10 *peppercorns*
　　　　 salt

Put the meat, 3 tablespoons of chopped onion, wine, vegetables and spices into an earthenware dish just large enough to accommodate it all, cover and let it stand overnight in a cool place.

The next day take the meat out of the marinade, strain the marinade, remove the bay leaves, mash the vegetables and set aside.

Pat the meat dry with paper towels and tie it with kitchen string so that it keeps its shape.

Heat the oil in a saucepan, add the remaining onions, the garlic and the meat and, turning the meat several times, let it brown on all sides. Add the mashed vegetables, lower the flame and simmer on a medium heat, turning it a few times.

When all the pan juices are absorbed pour the strained marinade over the meat. Cover the saucepan, lower the heat and continue to cook very slowly for three hours.

The meat should be so tender that it can be cut with a spoon.

Take the meat out of the saucepan, remove the string and put the meat on a preheated serving dish.

Remove the fat that has formed on the sauce, reheat the sauce and pour it over the meat. Carve at the table.

Serves 6

Beef Sausage or Luganega

I was given this recipe by the grandmother of my friend Miriam when I was staying with her in Venice about 37 years ago. I vividly remember the occasion when I was introduced to Luganega.

Miriam's grandmother, Signora Margherita, was at home. A tall, stately old lady, she couldn't possibly have been as ancient as she seemed to me at the time. My friend and I, and several very elegant, haughty-looking ladies were sipping coffee, sitting stiffly on spindly, straight-backed chairs.

Signora Margherita was holding forth about the correct way of making Luganega, a dish that must never be entrusted to the cook, a dish that she, Signora Margherita, always made herself according to the recipe passed on for generations in her family.

When one of the ladies dared to contradict Signora Margherita's instructions of how Luganega should be prepared, Signora Margherita excused herself and left the room.

A few minutes later the door opened and Signora Margherita came sailing into the room. Dressed in black, her jingoistic proportions majestic, her coiffured head held high, this stately, handsome apparition held, at arm's length, dangling from her heavily ringed fingers—a long, plump and odorous sausage.

The same evening Luganega was served for dinner. I must have made the right comments because, when my visit with my friend came to an end and I had said my goodbyes to Signora Margherita, she munificently handed me The Recipe for The Luganega, with strict instructions to pass it on to my future children.

By trial and error I have worked out the quantities for this recipe. They work well, however, for the sake of interest here are the quantities as given to me by Signora Margherita: 5 kg meat, 2 kg fat, 25 cloves garlic, 500 g salt, 200 g pepper, 200 g pepper kernels!!!

INGREDIENTS:

    700 g lean beef

    300 g fat, the fat should be taken from around the kidneys as this has a much firmer texture than other beef fat

    4–5 cloves garlic

    20 g salt
     4 g ground pepper
     4 g pepper kernels

Mince the meat, together with the fat, add the seasoning, mix well with a wet hand, then put the mixture through the mincer two more times.

Stuff the mixture into a length of perfectly clean intestine (derma).

However, if you want to avoid the tedious business of stuffing, wet both hands with cold water and form a thin, long sausage.

The long sausage can then be cut into sausage lengths and fried in very little oil or, it can be cut into small bits and cooked in soup, with beans, risotto and other dishes.

The sausages are tastier after a few days but without the casing they should not be kept too long.

Stuffed Cabbage for Simchat Torah

INGREDIENTS:

    12 cabbage leaves of the same size
   400 g finely minced yearling veal
     2 tablespoons bread crumbs sprinkled with stock
        or
     1 cup cold boiled rice
     1 cup tomato purée
     ½ cup olive oil
     1 small finely chopped onion
     1 egg
        stock
        freshly ground pepper
        salt

Immerse the cabbage leaves in boiling salt water for 2 minutes, then place the leaves flat on a working surface.

Working with one leaf at a time spread the leaf, cut out the hard centre and lay the two halves of the leaf so that they overlap a little where the centre is missing.

In a mixing bowl amalgamate the meat with the breadcrumbs or rice, and the egg, and season with salt and pepper to taste.

Divide the mixture into twelve parts, place one portion on each leaf then close the leaf as you would a parcel and wind a white cotton thread once or twice around the parcel to keep it closed.

In a shallow saucepan, wide enough to accommodate the cabbage parcels in one layer, heat the oil, add the onion and fry until the onion is light brown. Add the tomato purée and the cabbage rolls and enough stock to cover the rolls. Cover the saucepan, lower the heat and simmer slowly. The cabbage rolls should be ready when the juices are reduced to a tasty thick tomato sauce.

Transfer the rolls, one at a time, to a preheated serving dish, remove the strings carefully, pour the tomato sauce over the rolls and serve piping hot.

Serves 6

Editor's note: Cabbage rolls are more usually thought of as a Middle European dish, but they exist in every country where there is cabbage. They are traditional for Simhat Torah and for Succot, no doubt because cabbages were plentiful during the harvest season, but also because 'stuffed' foods suggest fullness. The symbolism of the round shape is also important, because it signifies a seamless continuity. Simhat Torah, the Rejoicing of the Law, is the festival when the last verses of the Torah (the five books of Moses) are read in the synagogue and the reading re-commences with the first verses of the first book, Genesis.

Hamin Toscano

This is a very old Tuscan recipe for minced meat balls. It is a rather complicated way to prepare minced meat but well worth the trouble— it really is delicious. Hamin is traditionally a winter dish.

INGREDIENTS:

　　　1　kg brisket of beef
　500　g lean minced beef
　　　6　beef sausages (see page 115)
　1.5　g turnips peeled and diced
　700　g brown beans
　　　2　eggs

    2 *hard-boiled eggs*
2–3 *slices crustless, white bread*
       olive oil
       freshly ground pepper
       salt

Fry the turnip cubes lightly, drain and set aside.

Put the beans in a saucepan, add enough water to cover the beans and enough oil to cover the surface of the water (the oil prevents the beans splitting), bring to the boil, cover the saucepan, lower the heat and continue to boil slowly for one hour.

After an hour raise heat, add the turnip and the brisket to the beans, cover with hot water, bring to the boil. Lower the heat, cover the saucepan, and continue to simmer for six or seven hours.

While the beans are cooking prepare the meat balls. Heat a saucepan with water with two tablespoons of oil. Wet your hand with cold water and knead together the minced meat, soaked bread, eggs, salt and pepper. When it is well amalgamated form round balls about the size of a walnut.

In a small saucepan bring to the boil salted water with three tablespoons of olive oil.

Put the meatballs into the boiling water (there should be enough water to cover the meat balls) and continue to boil until the meat balls are cooked, about fifteen to twenty minutes. When the meat balls are ready, drain and set them aside.

About twenty minutes before serving remove the brisket from the saucepan, cut it into chunks and return it to the saucepan together with the meatballs, the sausages and continue to simmer until you are ready to serve.

Put everything into a well-heated earthenware serving dish, taking care to arrange the meat, sausages and meat balls in rows next to each other. Slice the hard boiled eggs and arrange them around the dish.

Serve piping hot with lots of fresh crusty bread.

Serves 6

Editor's note: Hamin is the Italian version of the long-cooked dish traditionally served on the Sabbath. It is known as cholent by Eastern Europeans, dafina by Maroccan Jews, and hamin in Hebrew. There are all kinds of other names, and innumerable variations, but this is basically a mixture of meat, vegetables and pulses that solves the problem of how to eat a hot meal on the Sabbath when cooking is prohibited.

In former days, each family would have taken a pot to the baker, and left in the baker's oven from before sunset on Friday until it was time to eat it for lunch on Saturday. The fire would have been lit in the oven before Sabbath, and left to burn itself out. The heat would have been quite sufficient to cook everything.

In places where there was no baker's oven, a hay box would have been used. Everything would have been placed in the pot, brought to the boil simmered for a while, then placed in a box surrounded by hay. The hay provides enough insulation to enable the pot to stay hot. It would not have been very hot by Saturday lunchtime, but it would have still been quite warm enough to be palatable.

It is probably better to cook this in a slow oven overnight than on top of the stove. It is certainly better to eat it in the middle of the day because it can be seriously indigestible if it is eaten in the evening.

Minced Meats

I seem to have collected more variations of recipes for minced meat than any other cuts of meat. This is so because meat in Italy has always been expensive. Prime cuts of meat were considered the food of the 'Signoria' (gentle folk), whilst the cheap, tough parts of the animal were minced together with a lot of fat. A little minced meat goes very far for a pasta sauce if one is clever, just as the addition of stale bread makes rissoles go a long way.

During the early '50s, when I lived in Italy, even the families of the middle class ate meat only on Sundays and, I am told that this has not changed in southern Italy.

Nonna Rina and my sisters-in-law taught me to buy a cut of meat of their choice to be minced at home. The butcher was not to be trusted to mince good lean meat, nor could the cleanliness of the butcher's hand-operated mincer be trusted because he certainly minced non-kosher meats in the same machine. During my last visit, in 1985, I noticed a great change in butcher shops—they are clean and have modern appliances—but the price of meat is still very high and, unlike many other parts of Italy where the Jewish communities are larger, there are no kosher butchers in Naples and meat still has to be made kosher in the home. Another rule that I was taught was to calculate 100 g of meat per person when shopping for meat. I must admit that I lost that habit with great pleasure when we settled in Melbourne.

Editor's note: There may be another reason for the prevalence of minced meat recipes in a Jewish kitchen. Kosher meat, because it must be salted before cooking, tends to be tough. Mincing it makes it much more palatable. The many combinations of minced meat and vegetables given here are characteristic of Italian-Jewish cooking, and may result from the need to stretch the amount of meat to feed as many people as there were at the table. But the addition of vegetables introduces a great range of flavours to what might otherwise be a rather dull staple dish.

Minced Meatballs with Zucchini

Although I only have this and the following recipes in my collection, meatballs can be made with many other vegetables. In Rome I have tasted meatballs with finely chopped green peppers, in Florence I was served minced meatballs with cabbage, in Milan my cousin learned to make them with fennel. The vegetables are always precooked. Naturally, each vegetable gives the meatballs a different taste, and makes the humble meatball more interesting.

INGREDIENTS:
400 g sliced zucchini
250 g chopped onions
400 g finely minced beef
4–5 tablespoons bread crumbs
2 eggs
olive oil
flour
freshly ground pepper
salt

Boil the zucchini and chopped onions in salt water and, when soft, drain the zucchini and onions and leave them in the sieve to cool.

When the zucchini are cold, put them into a mixing bowl with the meat, eggs, bread crumbs, salt and pepper and mix until well amalgamated.

While mixing the meat wash your hands several times to remove the fat that sticks to them.

Form little meat balls, roll them in flour and fry in hot oil.

Serves 4

Minced Meatballs with Eggplant

The more oil there is in the frying pan and the hotter the oil is, the less oil the eggplant will absorb.

INGREDIENTS:

500 g finely minced beef
4 tablespoons bread crumbs
1 large eggplant, peeled and diced
2 cloves crushed garlic
2 chopped onions
2 eggs
olive oil
bread crumbs
freshly ground pepper
salt

Heat the oil in a frying pan and fry the onions until they are golden brown.

Remove the frying pan from the flame, remove the onions with a slotted spoon and spread them on several layers of kitchen towel to drain. Cover with more paper towels and pat as dry as you can.

Add more oil to the frying pan, heat well and add the garlic and eggplant pieces and fry, stirring frequently, until the eggplant is quite dark on all sides.

Discard the garlic cloves. Remove the eggplant from the oil with a slotted spoon, spread the eggplant on several layers of kitchen towel, cover with more paper towels and pat as dry as you can.

When the onions and eggplant are cold put them into a mixing bowl, add the meat, eggs, bread crumbs, salt and pepper and work until it is well amalgamated.

With wet hands form meatballs. Roll each meatball in bread crumbs and fry in ample hot oil, drain and serve hot or cold.

Serves 4

Minced Meatballs with Leeks

INGREDIENTS:

> *500 g lean minced beef*
> *1 tablespoon plain flour*
> *2 bunches (6) small leeks*
> *3 eggs*
> *olive oil*
> *freshly ground pepper*
> *salt*

Cut off and discard the green part of the leeks, then wash the remaining white and yellow parts and boil in salted water till tender.

Drain and cool the boiled leeks, squeeze dry, and when all the moisture is eliminated, chop finely, by hand or in the food processor.

In a mixing bowl blend the meat with the chopped leeks, eggs and flour, check the mixture for seasoning and add salt and pepper to taste.

Wet your hands with cold water and shape little meatballs about the size of walnuts.

Heat the oil in a frying pan and fry the meatballs over a brisk flame so that they brown quickly.

Serve hot or cold.

Serves 6

Zia Tilde's Minced Meatballs

This was Zia Tilde's favourite minced meat recipe. She claimed it as her own creation, even though using lamb instead of veal is not as original as she would have us believe.

INGREDIENTS:

    750 g ground lean minced lamb
    500 g ripe tomatoes peeled, seeded and cut into pieces
    100 g pine nuts
      1 teaspoon dry basil
        or
  3–4 leaves of fresh basil
      8 onions sliced whole to form rings
        olive oil
        flour
        freshly ground pepper
        salt

Ask your butcher to bone and mince the lean part only of a leg of lamb.

Season the meat with salt and pepper to your taste, add the pine nuts and mix the meat with your hand. Wash off the fat that sticks to your hand several times.

Form little meatballs then roll each meatball in flour and fry in hot oil, on a brisk heat, until golden brown all over.

Remove the meatballs from the frying pan and put them on several layers of kitchen towel to drain off as much oil as possible.

In the meantime put a little of the oil that was used for frying the meat into a saucepan, heat the oil and fry the onion rings.

When the onion rings are golden brown add the meatballs, the tomatoes, the basil and a pinch of salt and pepper. Cover the pan, lower the heat and cook slowly, stirring occasionally with a wooden spoon to avoid sticking, for about an hour.

The tomatoes should be reduced to the consistency of a not too thick sauce.

Serves 6

Meat Loaf in Dressing Gown

Pastry and filling can be prepared in advance but, do not roll them before you are ready to bake. Once the roll is baked keep it hot, do not reheat.

INGREDIENTS:

> *puff pastry, see recipe page 46*
> *or*
> *pasta limpada, see recipe page 54*
> *or*
> *pasta brisé, see recipe page 49*

> *Filling:*
> 400 *g minced boiled beef*
> 100 *g sultanas*
> 100 *g pine nuts*
> 3 *tablespoons olive oil*
> 1 *tablespoon water*
> 1 *egg*
> 1 *chopped onion*
> *freshly ground pepper*
> *salt*

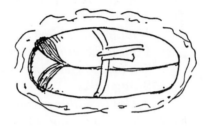

Prepare the pastry of your choice and set aside.

Heat the oil in a saucepan, add the onion and fry. When the onion is golden brown add the meat, egg, water, salt and pepper and, stirring frequently, simmer for 10 to 15 minutes.

Preheat the oven to 350°F or 180°C.

Roll out the pastry so that it forms a rectangle. Place the filling along the long side of the rectangle about five centimetres from the edge, lift the edge of the pastry and roll the filling into the pastry, then fold and pinch both ends firmly closed.

Place the finished roll on an oiled baking tray, brush the top of the pastry with a little oil, and bake until the pastry is golden brown.

Editor's note: The use of pine nuts and sultanas here suggests an Arabic origin.

Nonna Rina's Minced Meat Loaf

Nonna Rina's minced loaf was a great favourite with the family. The rosemary gives it a special flavour and the different shape makes it more interesting than other minced meat loaves.

Zia Tilde told me that this recipe was her creation, but Nonna Rina said that when she (Nonna Rina) was a little girl, her mother prepared the minced meat loaf according to this recipe.

INGREDIENTS:

> *600 g minced yearling beef*
> *2 tablespoons goose fat*
> *or*
> *2 tablespoons chicken fat*
> *or*
> *1 tablespoon olive oil*
> *1 tablespoon rosemary, crushed*
> *½ a loaf of Italian bread, crust removed*
> *2 egg yolks*
> *2 cloves garlic, chopped finely*
> *freshly ground pepper*
> *salt*
>
> *Sauce:*
> *1 425 g tin tomato purée*
> *2 tablespoons chopped parsley*
> *4 tablespoons olive oil*
> *1 teaspoon dry basil*
> *1 clove garlic, crushed*
> *freshly ground pepper*
> *salt*

Soak the bread in water or stock, squeeze dry and put it into a mixing bowl with the minced meat, salt and pepper and the egg yolks. Mix until well amalgamated.

Put the meat mixture into an oiled baking dish, and press it down firmly with your hand until the meat is about 3 cm high. Brush the top of the meat with oil and sprinkle it liberally with rosemary and chopped garlic. Bake in a moderate oven until the meat forms a golden crust.

Whilst the meat is cooking, prepare the sauce. Heat the oil in a saucepan, add the garlic and remove it as soon as it is golden brown, add the tomato purée, bring to the boil and lower the heat. Simmer uncovered, stirring occasionally, until the sauce becomes quite thick.

When both the sauce and the meat are ready, transfer the meat to a warmed serving dish, pour the pan juices from the baking dish into the tomato sauce, stir and pour over the meat.

Serve surrounded by boiled potatoes.

Serves 6

Pizzette of Heart

When my mother returned to Zagreb, after the war, a young man carrying a battered brown paper parcel came to visit her. The man introduced himself as the son of Mama's seamstress. He explained that he had fought with the partisans and that, on his recent return home, he was told by neighbours that his mother had died some time ago. He found his home looted and vandalised but, in the hiding place where his mother used to keep her money, he found this parcel with a note written by his mother. The note explained that in December 1942 before she was deported to the Concentration Camp, my grandmother asked his mother to safeguard this parcel. When he was told that Mama had come back, he brought her the parcel. The parcel contained the large embossed biscuit tin which Dad had given Mama during their engagement. What Mama had kept in the box before the war I do not know, but when in 1959 Mama came to Melbourne she brought the box with her and gave it to me.

Between the old photographs, letters and documents that were in the box when I received it I found this recipe. The recipe was written in Italian; it was scribbled on several crumpled and torn pieces of very thin paper. On the top of the first page was the date—Ancona, February 1809 and the remark 'Good for Succot'. I deciphered and copied the recipe faithfully but I am sorry to say that I have lost the original.

For the sake of interest I include the original recipe in this collection. I have translated it literally.

YOU WILL NEED:

> *a nice piece of veal*
> *a large ox heart*
> *a few handfuls of bread crumbs*
> *a measure of well-washed parsley which you will chop finely*
> 8 *artichokes which you will trim and wash as usual*
> 6 *fresh chicken eggs*
> 5 or 6 *cloves of good garlic that you will squash and chop very finely after you have peeled it*
> *a reasonable quantity of light olive oil*
> 10 *peppercorns which you must beat to powder with your heavy pestle*
> *a helping of kitchen salt that you have ground finely*

On the day before you wish to serve your pizzette, start your cooking early in the morning. To give the pizzette the right flavour you must use all the fat that you will find around the heart. You must chop the veal and the heart and the fat for at least one hour until they are so fine that you can push everything through your medium-size sieve. When you are satisfied that you have achieved this and nothing remains in the sieve, you may continue the preparation.

Put the sieved mass and all the other ingredients except the artichokes, into your large earthenware bowl. Now you must wash your hands thoroughly and make sure that you rinse off all the soap with freshly drawn water.

Proceed to knead the mass for half an hour so that the meat can absorb the aroma of the spices. Taste the mixture before you stop kneading and, if you think that the mixture is not well spiced, add the spice which you believe is missing and continue to knead until you are satisfied with the taste.

The next step is to wash your hands again, mind you use freshly drawn water for the rinsing of your hands. With wet hands take a fistful of meat and, rolling the meat between the palms of your hands, make a ball the size of a newborn baby's fist. Flatten each ball evenly into the shape of a pizzetta not thicker than a child's finger and place it in your large crock, into which you have poured a little oil, so that the pizzette lie on the bottom of the crock and not on top of each other. When all the pizzette are in the crock, pour enough oil into the crock to cover the pizzette completely.

Now cover the crock with the lid that fits best and put your covered crock on the window sill after you have wiped the sill with a clean wet rag. When you have placed the crock securely—so that it can not fall and hurt a child playing under the window—put your heaviest flat iron on the lid of your crock so that no animals can get at the meat. If you have no window that faces north, put the crock into the food cellar. Leave the crock on the window sill or in the cellar until the next morning.

Now you can begin with the preparation of your artichokes which you will wash and cut as you usually do when you braise them as a vegetable dish.

When the artichokes are ready, put some oil into the medium-sized good pot and put it onto the front of the stove to heat. When you are certain that your oil is hot put your artichokes into the hot oil and stir the artichokes with your wooden spoon. When you see that all the artichokes are well oiled and are beginning to sizzle, pour over them a little stock. Now cover your pot with a good lid and push it to the back of the stove so that it can simmer slowly where the heat is not high. Every little while check the artichokes and stir them around the pot with a clean wooden spoon, and when they are as tender as you like them, take the saucepan off the stove and place it in a cool place until the next morning when you are ready to finish cooking the pizzette.

Next morning bring the crock with the pizzette back into the kitchen. Prepare a grid which you have placed on a tin tray, take the pizzette out of the oil and arrange them on the grid to drain, and put the oil that you will have left in the crock into a clean jar so that you can use it again for another meat dish.

Take a wide, low pot and put the drained pizzette into the bottom of the pot and then put the artichokes on top of the pizzette. Put the pot on the stove, the stove must be hot already, and pour a little more of your good beef stock into the saucepan. Watch the pot until it begins to boil, when it does so, push it to the back of the stove where the heat is low and let it cook very slowly until you are ready to send it to the table.

Braised Leg of Lamb

I was given this recipe by an old friend who lived in Milano. However, when I served it in Napoli I was told, in no uncertain way, that it is an original Florentine dish.

It really does not matter where the recipe comes from because it is delicious. Leaving the vegetables to cook with the meat until the meat is ready, gives both the meat and the sauce a very special taste.

The vegetables can be varied according to the season, but I always use pumpkin, carrot, parsnip and celery as the basic vegetables because they give good colour and texture.

INGREDIENTS:

> 1.2 *kg leg of lamb*
> ½ *cup olive oil*
> 2 *cups stock*
>   *pumpkin*
> 2 *small zucchini*
>   *a few broccoli florettes*
> 1 *parsnip*
> 2 *carrots*
> 2 *celery stalks*
> 1 *onion*
> 5 *stalks parsley*
> 1 *glass dry white wine*
>   *freshly ground pepper*
>   *salt*

Cut the vegetables into large chunks and set aside.

Heat the oil in a large oval saucepan and put the meat into the hot oil turning it until it is sealed on all sides.

Remove the meat from the saucepan and set aside.

Put all the vegetables into the saucepan in which you sealed the meat, stir fry for a few minutes, lower the flame and allow the vegetables to brown slowly.

When the vegetables are well coloured, move the vegetables to the sides of the saucepan and return the meat, placing it in to the middle of the vegetables. Add the pan juices that have accumulated in the dish in which the meat was resting.

Lower the flame and simmer slowly until the pan juices disappear. Add the wine, cover the saucepan and continue to simmer slowly until all the wine has evaporated. When there is no more wine left add the stock, a little at a time, and continue to cook slowly until the meat is tender.

When ready, the meat should have a dark colour and the pan juices with the vegetables should have disintegrated so as to form a thick sauce.

Remove the meat from the saucepan and, after it has rested for 10 minutes, carve it and place the slices on a preheated serving dish. Mash the vegetables adding a little stock if the sauce is too thick, pour the sauce over the meat and serve.

Serves 5-6

Lamb or Baby Goat Roast

This is one of the most popular spring dishes in Rome. In 1953 and '54, Sandro, a very dear friend of ours, worked in Rome and came home to Napoli every weekend. During the three months of spring, every Saturday evening Sandro arrived at our doorstep, handed me an entire little dressed lamb, minus the head but always with the tail intact, and hurried home to his mother.

On Sunday morning I cooked dinner and of course roasted the lamb. Promptly at 2 o'clock I served 'The Sunday Dinner'. I can still see the dining table set and Sandro, two or three other friends, Riccardo with Mickie in his high chair next to him, all faces eagerly turned to the door through which the maid brought in the large dish with the roast.

There was usually a mixed antipasto, then lasagna or some other pasta dish, then the lamb served whole, surrounded by little young potatoes sprinkled with lots of parsley, followed by tossed green salad, fruit, assorted cheeses, coffee and a cake. Not to mention the wine. Today I wonder where we put it all. It was quite normal for dinner to last until 5 o'clock.

At any other time that I cooked baby lamb or goat I had the butcher bone the meat but I must admit that it never tasted quite as delicious as the whole animal.

INGREDIENTS:

>   *1.5 kg boned leg of lamb or baby goat*
>   *3-4 cloves garlic cut into slivers*
>   *fresh or dry rosemary*
>   *½ cup olive oil*
>   *freshly ground pepper*
>   *salt*

Rub the meat with garlic and rosemary, salt and pepper on both sides then roll it and tie with kitchen string.

Put the meat into a baking dish, together with 1 cup of water, pour the oil over the meat and bake, in a preheated oven at 350°F or 180°C. Baste frequently with the pan juices, until tender. When the meat is ready, remove it from the baking dish and allow to rest for about 10 minutes before removing the string and slicing.

Remove all the fat from the pan juices, then pour the pan juices into a small saucepan and bring to the boil, add the wine and boil briskly until the wine evaporates. Serve the sauce in a sauce boat.

Passover Lamb Stew with Eggs

Be very careful with the sauce, keep the double boiler on a low flame, because if the sauce comes to the boil it will curdle.

INGREDIENTS:

>   *1 kg cubed lamb*
>   *½ cup olive oil*
>   *4 eggs*
>   *juice of 1 lemon*
>   *stock*
>   *2 crushed garlic cloves*
>   *pinch rosemary*
>   *freshly ground pepper*
>   *salt*

In a saucepan, heat the oil, add the garlic and remove it when it is golden brown, add the meat cubes and stir fry until the meat is well sealed, then season with salt and pepper, lower the flame, add a little stock, cover and simmer slowly until the meat is tender.

Add a little stock when needed so that the meat is kept moist during the whole cooking time.

When the meat is ready put it into a preheated serving dish and keep it very hot.

Beat the eggs with the lemon juice, salt and pepper until amalgamated then, beating continually, cook in a double boiler until the sauce thickens a little.

Pour the sauce over the hot meat and serve immediately.

Editor's note: The egg and lemon sauce in this dish suggests a Sephardi origin. The following recipe, too, may well be Sephardi in origin.

Serves 4-6

Cubed Passover Lamb with Lemon

This is a very nice and easy dish to prepare, therefore popular at Passover when there is always so much to do.

INGREDIENTS:

> 1.2 *kg cubed lamb*
> 1 *cup chopped parsley*
> ½ *cup olive oil*
> 4-5 *cloves garlic with skin*
> *stock*
> *juice of 1-2 lemons*
> *freshly ground pepper*
> *salt*

Heat the oil in a saucepan and when it is hot add the unpealed garlic cloves and fry until the garlic cloves are golden brown, add the cubed meat and continue to stir fry till the meat is well sealed and brown.

Add a little stock, the parsley, salt and pepper, cover, lower the flame, and simmer for about half an hour, or until the meat is tender, adding a little stock when needed.

When ready put the meat with its pan juices on a preheated serving dish, sprinkle with the lemon juice and serve very hot.

Serves 6

Shoulder of Lamb with Olives

This is an easy dish to prepare, very popular in Rome as well as in Milan.

INGREDIENTS:

>   1 *kg boned rolled shoulder of lamb*
> 100 *g pitted halved green olives*
>   6 *tablespoons olive oil*
>   1 *teaspoon thyme*
>   1 *cup stock*
>   3 *sliced carrots*
>   3 *sliced medium onions*
>   1 *laurel leaf*
>   2 *cloves*
>   *freshly ground pepper*
>   *salt*

Heat the oil in a heavy saucepan, add the meat and turn it until it is golden brown all over, add the carrots, onions, thyme, laurel leaf, cloves, salt, pepper and hot stock.

Bring to the boil, cover, lower the flame, and simmer slowly until the meat is tender.

Add the olives 15–20 minutes before the end of cooking time.

Serves 6

Stuffed Turkey Neck Alla Romana

This recipe, as it was given to me, advises putting a rack on a large soup plate, placing the neck on the rack, covering it and leaving it overnight on the window sill, but to be careful the cats do not get it! Rome was always famous for its innumerable stray cats.

INGREDIENTS:

> 1 *skin of turkey neck*
> 2 *chicken or turkey livers*
> 2 *eggs*
> 1 *hard-boiled egg*

½ *cup rice*
   or
3 *tablespoons fresh bread crumbs*
2 *tablespoons chopped pine nuts*
   olive oil
   freshly ground pepper
   salt

The skin of the turkey must be clean, with no feathers or other impurities adhering to it. Rinse the skin in cold water, pat it dry with a paper towel and set it aside.

On a brisk flame sauté the livers in a little oil, remove from the flame and allow to cool, then mince in a meat mincer, not a food processor, as the texture should be chunky, not a smooth paste.

Chop the hard-boiled egg and add it to the liver, together with the raw eggs, bread crumbs or rice and pine nuts. Season with salt and pepper and mix lightly until all the ingredients are amalgamated.

With needle and white thread carefully stitch the skin together on one side, then fill the skin with the prepared mixture and stitch together the other end of the skin, taking care that you do not tear the skin. Pierce the stuffed skin in several points with a meat skewer or the point of a very sharp knife, again carefully, so as not to tear the skin.

Put the stuffed neck into a saucepan, cover it with water and bring it to the boil, then lower the flame, cover and cook very slowly for an hour and a half. When cooked, remove the neck from the water, place it on a rack, cover, and refrigerate overnight.

To serve, slice the neck as you would slice a salami, but thicker. Serve with eggplant in vinegar, see page 167.

Editor's note: Stuffed poultry necks are more common in Eastern European Jewish cooking. This is obviously a festival dish, because it must be made ahead of time.

Nonna Rina's Turkey Loaf

Because of the time-consuming preparation, and the beautiful marbled look of the slices, the turkey loaf is a favourite Holiday dish in Italian Jewish homes.

To cool under weight: put the loaf into a deep, flat bottomed dish, cover it with a flat plate and put a heavy weight onto the plate. My mother-in-law used a flat iron for the weight. I use two 750 g tins.

INGREDIENTS:

2 kg turkey breast, whole with unbroken skin
500 g veal
soup bones
150 g chicken
or
150 g turkey fat
1 cup pine nuts
or
1 cup pistachio nuts
3 sprigs parsley
½ celery stalk
small onion
small carrot
1 crushed garlic clove
pinch grated nutmeg
freshly ground pepper
salt

Prepare the stock at least a day in advance. Remove the skin from the turkey breast, very carefully, without damaging it. Bone the turkey breast leaving the meat whole. In a large saucepan boil the turkey bones, soup bones, carrot, parsley, celery, onion, a little salt and pepper and enough water to make sufficient stock to cook the turkey loaf in. When the stock is ready, sieve it, cool it and refrigerate it overnight.

Next day cut the turkey meat into slices, lengthways, to form long strips about the thickness of a finger, cut the veal the same way but cut the chicken fat thinner than the strips of meat.

Prepare a thick needle with a long, double thread of white cotton.

Now spread the skin, inside out, flat on the working surface and rub gently with the crushed garlic.

Alternating the turkey and veal strips and adding an occasional strip of fat, form layers, arranging the strips lengthways on one half of the open skin, and leaving about 2 cm of skin free on the other three sides around the meat. Sprinkle each layer with pine nuts and a little salt and pepper.

If there is too much filling it is better to remove some, because if the skin is too full it will burst while cooking. To avoid all danger of the skin breaking, the finished loaf can be rolled into a piece of cheese cloth which can be removed before slicing the loaf when it is ready to be served.

When all the meat strips are in place, fold the empty half of the skin over the meat and stitch the skin together around the three open sides. Keep the stitches as close to each other as you can but be very careful not to tear the skin by pulling the stitches too hard.

When the skin is stitched pierce it in several places with a thick needle so that it will not burst while cooking, and refrigerate it overnight.

The next day remove the fat that will have formed on top of the stock and if the stock has jellied, melt it over a low heat without allowing it to become hot. Put the turkey loaf into the saucepan with the cool stock, bring to the boil, cover, lower the flame, and cook slowly for two and a half hours.

Remove the loaf from the stock, cool the stock and keep it for future use. Put the loaf on an inverted soup plate and let it cool, then refrigerate it under weight for several hours, preferably overnight.

Before you cut the loaf, scrape off all the stock that may have jellied around it, do this carefully because the cooked skin tears very easily. Slice across the width of the loaf, cutting the slices about 2 cm thick. Arrange the slices on a flat serving dish and garnish with sprigs of parsley.

Zia Tilde's Turkey Loaf

Zia Tilde's turkey loaf is much easier to prepare than Nonna Rina's turkey loaf but, although the taste of the two loaves is very similar, their texture and appearance are very different. Nonna Rina's version is by far my favourite recipe.

INGREDIENTS:

　　　2　*kg turkey breast, whole*
　500　*g finely minced veal*
　150　*g minced chicken fat*
　　　　or
　150　*g minced turkey fat*
　　　3　*eggs*
　　　3　*hard-boiled eggs*
　　　　soup bones
　　　3　*sprigs parsley*
　　½　*celery stalk*
　　　　small onion
　　　　finely crushed garlic
　　　　pinch of grated nutmeg
　　　　freshly ground pepper
　　　　salt

Very carefully remove the skin from the turkey breast, without damaging it.

Bone the turkey carefully, and dice the meat.

In a largish saucepan boil the turkey bones, soup bones, carrot, parsley, celery, onion, a little salt and pepper and enough water to make sufficient stock to cook the turkey loaf in; when ready, sieve the stock and allow it to cool.

In a mixing bowl combine the diced turkey, minced veal, minced chicken fat, raw eggs, salt, pepper and nutmeg.

Prepare a thick needle with a long, double thread of white cotton.

Spread the skin, inside out, flat on the working surface and rub gently with the crushed garlic. Fold the skin over lengthways, garlic side inwards, and stitch it together leaving one narrow side open.

Be very careful not to tear the skin by pulling the stitches too hard and keep the stitches close to each other so that the filling cannot escape. Divide the filling into five more or less equal parts, put one part of the filling into the skin, then place one hard boiled egg on the filling and repeat until all the filling and all the eggs are in the skin, then, holding the filled skin upright, stitch together the remaining opening.

When the skin is stitched pierce it in several places with a thick needle, so that it will not burst in cooking, and place it in the cold stock, bring to the boil, cover, lower the flame, and cook slowly for two and a half hours.

When ready remove the loaf from the stock and cool it under weight, (see previous recipe), refrigerating it for several hours, preferably overnight.

Slice across the width of the loaf, making the slices about 2 cm thick, arrange the slices on a flat serving dish and garnish with sprigs of parsley.

Minced Turkey Patties with Celery

Dark meat should be used for the preparation of minced patties.

INGREDIENTS:

>   750 *g boned turkey, finely minced*
>   3 *tablespoons bread crumbs*
>   *or*
>   *bread soaked in stock*
>   3 *eggs*
>   2 *celery stalks, chopped*
>   *stock*
>   *olive oil*
>   *freshly ground pepper*
>   *salt*

Put the minced meat into a mixing bowl, add the eggs, bread crumbs or the bread soaked in stock and squeezed dry, salt and pepper, and work until the mixture is smooth and well amalgamated. Form small patties.

In a shallow saucepan fry the chopped celery in a little oil, put the meat patties on top of the celery, add 1 cup of stock, cover the saucepan, lower the flame, and simmer for about half an hour, adding more stock if needed.

The turkey patties are usually served with boiled new potatoes sprinkled with lots of fresh, finely chopped parsley.

Serves 6

Grilled Chicken Breast

INGREDIENTS:

> 2 *skinned chicken breasts*
> 2 *tablespoons olive oil*
> 2 *tablespoons lemon juice*
>   *freshly ground pepper*
>   *salt*

Put the chicken breasts into an earthenware or glass container in which they fit compactly.

Put the lemon juice, oil, salt and pepper into a shallow dish and beat with a fork until it is well amalgamated, then pour it over the chicken breasts.

Turn the chicken breasts once or twice, to make sure that they are well coated all over. Cover the dish and allow to stand for at least one hour.

Cook under a hot grill or on the barbecue for about 5 minutes on each side.

Serves 2

Fried Chicken

This recipe is a favourite Hanuckah dish because it involves frying, although it is generally used during the year.

INGREDIENTS:

> 1 *chicken size 12 cut into 4*
>   *or*
> 4 *chicken Maryland pieces*
> 2 *tablespoons olive oil*
> 2 *eggs*
>   *juice of one lemon*
>   *flour*
>   *olive oil*
>   *freshly ground pepper*
>   *salt*

Put the chicken pieces into an earthenware or glass container in which they fit compactly.

Put the lemon juice, oil, salt and pepper into a shallow dish and beat with a fork until well amalgamated, then pour it over the chicken.

Turn the chicken pieces once or twice to make sure that they are well coated on all sides, cover the dish and allow to stand for at least one hour.

Remove the chicken pieces from the marinade and pat dry with a paper towel.

Break the eggs into a soup plate, season with salt and pepper and beat lightly with a fork.

Coat the chicken pieces with flour, dip into the egg and fry in hot oil.

When the chicken is golden brown on all sides remove it from the oil and put it on a rack to drain in a moderately hot oven, leaving the oven door open, until you are ready to serve.

Serves 4

Zia Tilde's Chicken

INGREDIENTS:

> 1 *large roasting chicken cut into portions*
>   *or*
> 6 *Maryland portions*
> 1 *onion finely chopped*
> 1 *teaspoon rosemary*
> 1 *tablespoon flour*
> 1 *tablespoon tomato paste*
> 1½ *cups olive oil*
> 2 *cups chicken stock*
>   *freshly ground pepper*
>   *salt*

Heat one cup of oil in a wide, shallow saucepan, add the chicken pieces, forming only one layer, and fry on a low flame, turning the chicken frequently so that it browns evenly on all sides.

While the chicken is browning heat the remaining oil, add the onion and rosemary and fry until the onion is light brown.

In a small mixing bowl blend the flour with a little stock, mixing well to avoid lumps, add the tomato paste and the remaining stock and pour into the saucepan with the browned onion, mix with a wooden spoon and pour over the chicken pieces.

Continue to simmer on a low flame for about half an hour, turning the chicken and shaking the saucepan to avoid the sauce sticking.

Serves 6

Chicken with Green Peppers

Because of the green peppers used in this recipe, it is very often served for Succot instead of the stuffed cabbage leaves.

INGREDIENTS:

> *1.5 kg chicken cut into portions*
> *500 g peeled, chopped and seeded tomatoes*
> *500 g green peppers chopped*
> *100 g pitted black olives*
> *3 tablespoons olive oil*
> *3 onions finely chopped*
> *2 cloves crushed garlic*
> *chicken stock*
> *freshly ground pepper*
> *salt*

Heat the oil in a wide, shallow pan, pat the chicken pieces dry with a kitchen towel and fry, side by side, turning the pieces several times till they are well browned on all sides. Arrange the fried pieces on a plate and keep warm.

Reheat the oil in the saucepan, add the onion and garlic and, stirring with a wooden spoon, fry until the garlic is browned then remove and discard it.

Continue to fry the onion until it is brown. Add the peppers and tomatoes, salt and pepper, but be careful with the salt because the olives are salty, cover the pan, lower the flame and simmer for about an hour and a half.

Shake the saucepan frequently and turn the chicken pieces, adding a few tablespoons of stock if needed.

Add the olives half an hour before the chicken is ready.

Serves 4–5

Chicken in Liver Sauce

This is one of Virginia's special recipes. The original dish is really delicious but every time Virginia prepared it, she would substitute one ingredient for another or add a different spice, so that it never tasted exactly the same. The only ingredients that never varied were the chicken, the pickled onions and the liver.

INGREDIENTS:

1 kg chicken pieces
3 minced chicken livers
1 cup chicken stock
1 cup dry white wine
2 tablespoons olive oil
2 tablespoons chopped parsley
1 teaspoon dried basil
1 teaspoon dried oregano
15 pickling onions
20 chopped capers
1 carrot finely sliced
1 clove garlic, crushed
plain flour
freshly ground pepper
salt

Heat the oil in a saucepan, cover the chicken pieces with seasoned flour and fry briskly so that the chicken browns quickly on both sides, then add the onions, carrot, parsley, basil, oregano, salt and pepper, wine and stock, and bring to the boil. Cover the saucepan, lower the heat, and continue to simmer until the chicken is tender and the sauce well reduced.

When the chicken is ready, take it out of the sauce, arrange it on a preheated serving dish and keep it hot.

Put the chopped liver into the sauce, stir with a wooden spoon and continue to simmer for 10–15 minutes. Before removing the sauce from the heat add the capers, stir well and pour the sauce over the chicken pieces.

Serves 4

Disguised Boiler

This is an easy way to disguise a boiler after making a good, strong chicken soup.

INGREDIENTS:

> 1.2 *kg chicken*
> 100 *g reconstituted dry mushrooms*
> 1 *tablespoon plain flour*
> 1 *celery stalk*
> 1 *carrot*
> 1 *small onion*
> 3 *eggs*
>   *freshly ground pepper*
>   *salt*

Boil the chicken with the onion, celery, carrot, salt and pepper, the same way as you would cook it to make chicken soup.

When the chicken is very tender drain it and refrigerate the soup for future use.

Allow the chicken to cool a little then remove and discard all the skin, bones and fat.

Preheat the oven to 350°F or 180°C.

Cut the chicken into very small pieces, do not mince it or the texture will be mushy. Put the pieces into a mixing bowl, add the mushrooms, eggs and flour and mix it all together, season with salt and pepper.

Put the mixture into an oiled baking dish, preferably one with a hole in the middle.

Stand the baking tin in water and bake for one hour.

Unmould as soon as it is ready, and serve hot or cold, garnished with fresh parsley.

Chicken Loaf

The stock should be prepared a couple of days in advance and the loaf at least one day ahead of serving it. It is a very attractive and tasty dish. Like the turkey loaves, the chicken loaf is usually served on holidays.

INGREDIENTS:

>   1.5 *kg roasting chicken*
>   300 *g chicken breast*
>   300 *g veal*
>   50 *g goose salami*
>   30 *g pistachio nuts*
>   2 *eggs*
>   2 *hard-boiled eggs*
>   1 *truffle thinly sliced (optional)*
>   *olive oil*
>   *chicken stock*
>   *freshly ground pepper*
>   *salt*

Carefully remove the skin from the chicken.

The easiest way to skin a chicken is to cut off the neck, then whilst you lift the skin away from the flesh with one hand, gently pass the other hand between the skin and the flesh, until you have separated and removed all the skin.

Bone the chicken.

With a thick needle and white thread, stitch together the holes left by the drumsticks and wings and set the skin aside. In Venice it is the custom to leave the wings and drumsticks intact.

Cut all the chicken breasts and the veal into thin, long strips and sauté lightly in a little hot oil, then allow to cool.

Mince the remaining chicken, put it in a mixing bowl and combine with the eggs, goose salami, pistachio nuts, truffle, salt and pepper.

Place the skin flat on your working surface and, leaving 2 or 3 centimetres free around three edges, cover one half of the skin, lengthways, with half of the meat strips, alternating chicken and veal, then cover with half of the minced mixture. Put the hard-boiled eggs on top of the minced meat mixture, cover with the remaining half of the mixture, then cover this with the remaining strips of meat, again alternating chicken and veal.

Carefully fold the empty half of the skin over the filling and stitch together.

With a needle or with a sharp pointed knife, pierce the skin in several places.

Place the loaf in a saucepan, cover it with cold stock and bring it to the boil. Cover the saucepan, lower the flame, and cook slowly for about two and a half hours.

When ready, remove the loaf from the saucepan very carefully and allow it to cool in an inverted soup plate. When the loaf has cooled place it under weight (see recipe for Nonna Rina's Turkey Loaf, on page 136), and refrigerate at least overnight.

When ready to serve cut crossways into 2 cm slices and arrange on a flat serving dish garnished with sprigs of parsley.

Chicken in Aspic

To prepare a true aspic, see recipe on page 105 or, if you want a short-cut, follow this recipe.

INGREDIENTS:

> *1.2 kg boiling chicken*
> *2 celery stalks*
> *2 medium carrots*
> *1 onion*
> *freshly ground pepper*
> *salt*

Put the chicken with all the vegetables into a large saucepan with about three litres of cold water and bring it to the boil. Season with salt and pepper, cover the saucepan, lower the heat and continue to boil very slowly until more than two thirds of the water has evaporated.

Take the chicken out of the soup, and cut it into quarters.

Arrange the chicken pieces on a serving plate so that the pieces are lying flat without touching each other.

Drain the vegetables, set aside the carrots. Cut the carrots into thin slices and arrange these around the chicken.

Add a little gelatine to the clear soup and bring it to the boil again, then slowly pour the soup over the chicken.

Cover and refrigerate at least overnight before serving.

Serves 4

Stewed Goose Breast
An Ancient Venetian Recipe

INGREDIENTS:

1 whole goose breast boned, but with all the fat surrounding it
3 tablespoons tomato paste
2 cloves crushed garlic
  freshly ground pepper
  salt

Put the goose breast into a shallow pot in which the two pieces will fit side by side.

Sprinkle with salt and pepper, add the undiluted tomato paste, cover and cook, very slowly, over a low flame, for at least two or even three hours.

When the dish is ready, the fat will have melted, and the pan juices will have formed a very tasty gravy that will saturate the meat with the same flavour.

Zia Emma's Goose Salami

An old recipe from Ancona, still very popular in small communities where there are no kosher butchers.

The quantity of salt and pepper used for the salami in this recipe can be reduced, but not less than half should be used or the salami will spoil.

In Italy this salami is traditionally made in winter, not later than January.

If you have any of the minced mixture left over freeze it until you have a spare neck or add some finely chopped onion, form patties and grill. It is delicious!

INGREDIENTS:

1 3 kg fat goose
  for each 1 kg of meat and fat mixture:
30 g salt
5 g freshly ground pepper
5 g whole pepper kernels

After you have washed the goose thoroughly, use a small sharp knife to make an incision around the base of the neck, then carefully, without breaking it, pull the skin off the neck, and turn it inside out.

Carefully remove all the fat from the skin, again without tearing it. The skin must be clean, with no feathers or other impurities adhering to it. Rinse the skin well in cold water, sprinkle it liberally with salt all over and set it aside.

Cut off the wings and drumsticks and set them aside.

Remove all the skin from the carcass and bone it. Separate the fat from the meat. Mince the meat coarsely because, if the meat is cut into strips, it will make the salami rather tough. On the other hand, if it is minced finely the texture of the salami will not be very appealing. Put the minced meat into a large mixing bowl.

Take the skin from the carcass, spread it on the working surface and remove the film of thin outer skin which, when cooked, becomes very hard. Chop the skin and the fat coarsely.

Weigh the minced meat and the diced fat separately. There should be two thirds of meat and a generous third of fat. If you have too much fat, bone and mince the meat from the drumsticks and add it to the rest.

Put the minced meat, fat and skin, together with the seasoning, into a large mixing bowl and mix until it is well amalgamated.

Rinse the skin of the neck under cold running water then pat it dry with paper towels. Make sure that the inside of the skin is facing outward, and carefully stitch together the wider of the two openings.

Hold the skin upright, so that the stitched side rests on the working surface, and spoon the meat mixture into the skin, a little at a time, each time pressing the mixture down carefully so that no air pockets are formed.

When the skin is full, whilst still holding it upright, stitch together the open end of the skin and, with a thick needle, perforate the salami in several places to allow all air to escape.

Insert a strong toothpick halfway into each of the corners of the wider seam then, with thin white string, tie around the corners to form two 'ears', leaving enough string between the corners to form a handle by which the salami can be hung. Alternatively, forget about the toothpicks and string and put the salami into a cheesecloth bag, using the bag to hang the salami with.

Hang the salami in the kitchen for 24 hours, having placed a plate under it to catch the superfluous fat that will drip out. Then put the salami onto a working surface and press it well with your hands to remove any residual air bubbles.

Should the skin break, stitch it together again without disturbing the filling.

Now put the salami on a rack, cover it with gauze (not glad wrap because it must breathe) and put it into a cool, well-ventilated place, for two months.

Goose Prosciutto

This recipe is from Venice.

INGREDIENTS:

> 1 *large goose*
> *rock salt*
> *freshly ground pepper*
> *salt*

With a large, sharp knife and the help of a hammer, cut the goose along the backbone, or ask the butcher to do it for you, then spread the goose open, cut side down.

With a small, sharp knife cut around the drumstick and thigh and remove them in one piece with the skin intact.

Set aside the carcass.

Lay the drumsticks on the working bench with the underside facing you and bone it cutting from the top of the thigh lengthways down to the bottom of the drumstick.

Remove the bone, open the meat from the cut outward and rub salt and pepper into the meat.

Put a thick layer of rock salt on the bottom of a not too shallow earthenware dish and put one drumstick, skin down, on the salt, put the other drumstick on top, skin up, and cover well with more salt.

Place under weight (see recipe on page 136), and leave for 4 days, removing the liquid that will form around the meat every morning and every evening, and if there is no liquid before the 4 days are up, add more salt.

On the fifth day, with a thick needle and white double thread, stitch

together the skins working all around to form a shape resembling a
small prosciutto.

Sprinkle salt over the whole prosciutto, put it on a rack, cover it
with gauze (not glad wrap because it must breathe) and hang it in a
cool place for one or two months. Serve thinly sliced.

See the next recipe for the remaining parts of the goose.

Goose Breast

This recipe is actually a continuation of the previous one.

Having made the prosciutto you will have the carcass with all its
skin left over.

Remove the breast from the bone together with the skin, without
breaking the skin.

Put each breast flat on the working surface and cut away the surplus
skin, so that the meat looks like an open book.

Follow the recipe for the prosciutto (see previous recipe), and on
the fifth day fold each breast lengthways, like a closed book, and stitch
the skin together.

Continue as for the prosciutto.

After you have finished with the preparation of the breast, remove
the fat from the remaining skin, dice it and heat it on a low fire until
the fat melts and the remaining dice or 'cicoli' are golden.

Strain, use the fat for cooking and eat the cicoli, whilst still hot,
sprinkled with salt on fresh bread.

All that remains of the goose, bar the liver, can be made into a delicious
soup following the chicken soup recipe. For the preparation of the liver
see the next recipe.

Goose Liver

Remove all the fat from the liver and set aside.

Over an open flame singe the liver all over, carefully, so as not to
burn it. If you have no gas flame available, singe the liver over the
flame of a candle.

With a small, sharp knife make shallow, superficial cuts, lengthways on both sides of the liver. Put salt and pepper into all the cuts, then place the liver onto an upturned soup plate and leave it to drain for one hour.

Meanwhile dice the fat finely. Put it into a saucepan, together with the liver, and simmer very slowly, over low heat, for about 20 to 30 minutes, according to size.

Remove the liver from the saucepan and sprinkle it with bread crumbs all over. Remove half of the fat from the saucepan, return the liver to the saucepan and continue to cook slowly for another 15 minutes or so, but do not overcook the liver or it will become hard.

The liver is served hot, cut into thin slices and sprinkled with fresh, finely chopped parsley.

In Venice I was told that left-over liver is not usable as it can not be reheated; however in Zagreb, as well as in other parts of Europe, goose liver is never served hot!

Hence, if some of the liver is left over, put it into a deep dish, reheat the fat and pour it around the liver, with just a thin film of fat over the cut part. Refrigerated, the liver will keep for several weeks.

The cold liver is cut paper thin and eaten on a slice of bread.

Vegetables

In Italy, each course and dish is served separately so that meat and/
or fish are never served together with vegetables unless they form part
of the same dish. Only occasionally are meat or fish dishes served with
fried, baked or mashed potatoes. Salad, too, is served after the meat
or fish.

*Editor's note: The uses of vegetables in the Italian kitchen are among
its glories. The recipes that follow are only a selection of the riches
of Italian and Italian-Jewish vegetable cookery.*

Artichokes

*Editor's note: Artichokes are popular with Italians generally, Jewish or
not, but they were traditionally especially popular among Italian Jews
during Passover, when they come into season.*

Fried Artichokes

This is an old Roman recipe. Although artichokes are available all over Italy, they are particularly popular in Rome, and the rounded Roman artichoke is the most popular variety.

Once an artichoke is cut it should be either rubbed with lemon or soaked in lemon juice and icy water to prevent it becoming black. Rub your hands with lemon immediately after you have cut artichokes or your hands will be black, too.

INGREDIENTS:

> *1 artichoke per person*
> *olive oil for deep frying*
> *lemon juice*
> *chopped parsley*
> *freshly ground pepper*
> *salt*

To trim the artichokes, cut off the stem so that about three or four centimetres of stem remain attached to the head. Remove the hard outer leaves, and with a small, sharp knife cut off the top of the leaves to form a cone. Beat the artichokes gently against a chopping board to loosen the leaves.

Put the artichokes into a bowl with cold water, ice cubes and lemon juice, and allow to soak for a couple of hours.

Remove the artichokes from the water, shake as much water off them as possible, then dry with paper towels.

Open the leaves of the artichokes without detaching them from the centre core. Sprinkle salt, pepper and parsley between the leaves, and press the leaves together again.

Heat the oil, add the artichokes and, turning frequently, fry slowly until tender. Drain and serve hot.

Nonna Rina's Stuffed Artichokes

Stuffed artichokes are a very attractive buffet or luncheon dish. It is one of the dishes that Nonna Rina called 'elegant', and Zia Tilde claimed as her own concoction. Even the Venetian matriarch, La Signora Margherita, gave me a recipe for artichokes alternately filled with black and red caviar, served cold, on a bed of chopped hard-boiled eggs.

INGREDIENTS:

- 12 *artichokes*
- 150 *g chopped anchovy fillets*
- 50 *g rindless bread*
- 3 *tablespoons chopped parsley*
- 5 *tablespoons olive oil*
- 3 *finely chopped garlic cloves*
- *stock*
- *lemon juice*
- *freshly ground pepper*
- *salt*

Remove the stems from the artichokes so that they can rest on the bottom of a bowl without tipping over. Remove the hard outer leaves and the top of the remaining leaves.

Put the artichokes into a bowl of cold water with ice and lemon juice added and allow to soak for an hour or more.

Dip the bread in part of the stock, then squeeze dry. Put the bread into a mixing bowl together with the anchovies, garlic and parsley, season with salt and pepper and mix with a fork until well amalgamated.

Remove the artichokes from the lemon water, drain and dry with paper towel. With your fingers, gently open the centre of the artichokes without detaching the leaves from the core.

Divide the stuffing mixture into twelve portions and place one portion into each artichoke centre.

Arrange the stuffed artichokes in a saucepan, standing upright side by side. Add enough stock to reach about halfway up the sides of the artichokes, pour a generous trickle of oil on top of each artichoke, cover and bake for an hour in a preheated oven at 350°F or 180°C. Baste frequently with pan juices. Serve hot or cold.

Serves 6

Zia Emma's Stuffed Artichokes

INGREDIENTS:

 12 *artichokes*
 400 *g minced meat*
  4 *tablespoons chopped parsley*
  4 *eggs*
   olive oil
   freshly ground pepper
   salt

Remove the stems from the artichokes so that, when cooked, the artichokes can rest on the bottom of a pan without tipping over, remove the hard outer leaves and the top of the remaining leaves.

Put the artichokes into a bowl with cold water and lemon juice and soak for an hour or more.

In a mixing bowl combine the minced meat, parsley and two eggs and season with salt and pepper.

Remove the artichokes from the lemon water, drain and dry with paper towel. With your fingers, gently open the centre of each artichoke.

Divide the meat mixture into twelve portions and place one portion into each artichoke centre.

Beat the remaining two eggs in a small mixing bowl.

Heat a generous quantity of oil in a frying pan, dip each stuffed artichoke first into the beaten egg, then into the hot oil and fry until golden brown on both sides.

Use a slotted spoon to remove the fried artichokes from the oil and arrange them, in a preheated oven at low heat, on a rack in a baking dish so that they drain off oil, and at the same time remain hot until you are ready to serve.

Serves 6

Editor's note: When preparing any of the above recipes, be sure to remove all the tough outer leaves. Choose smaller, younger artichokes for preference.

Artichokes with Sauce

INGREDIENTS:

    8 *artichokes*
    2 *tablespoons chopped parsley*
    ½ *cup olive oil*
  2-3 *cups stock*
    3 *chopped cloves garlic*
     lemon juice
     freshly ground pepper
     salt

     Sauce:
    4 *egg yolks*
    4 *tablespoons olive oil*
    8 *tablespoons water*
    1 *teaspoon plain flour*
     juice of 1 lemon
     freshly ground pepper
     salt

Remove the outer leaves and the stems of the artichokes, cut off the top of the remaining leaves, then cut lengthways in half.

Put the artichokes into a bowl of cold water, with ice and lemon, and allow to soak for 1 hour.

Drain the artichokes and arrange them in a wide, shallow saucepan, open side up, side by side, in one layer. Sprinkle with salt, pepper, garlic, parsley and the oil, add half of the stock, cover and simmer over a low flame for about an hour, frequently basting and carefully turning the artichokes. If the pan juices evaporate add more stock, always only a little at a time.

When the artichokes are tender arrange them, side by side, open side up, on a wide serving dish and keep hot.

In a double boiler, blend together all the ingredients for the sauce with a wooden spoon. Put the double boiler on a medium heat and stir constantly until the sauce thickens, then pour it over the artichoke halves, sprinkle with chopped parsley and serve immediately.

Serves 4

Baked Artichokes with Veal

I have listed this dish under vegetables because of the artichokes, but it can be used as a first course as well as for a meat course, followed by a fresh salad. Kept on a hotplate it is a delicious buffet dish.

INGREDIENTS:

    6 *artichokes*
500 *g minced veal*
    1 *tablespoon nutmeg*
  ½ *cup olive oil*
     freshly ground pepper
     salt

Remove most of the stems and all the outer leaves of the artichokes, cut off the tops of the leaves so as to form a cone, and cut lengthways into thin wedges.

In a flame and ovenproof dish arrange the artichokes and veal in layers, beginning and ending with artichokes and sprinkling each layer with salt, pepper, nutmeg and a trickle of oil. Add water, till about halfway up the layers, cover the dish and simmer on low heat for about half an hour.

Preheat the oven to 350°F or 180°C, transfer the dish to the oven and bake, uncovered, for another half an hour. Serve hot.

Serves 4

Artichoke Hearts

INGREDIENTS:

12 *artichokes*
  3 *tablespoons chopped parsley*
  2 *cups stock*
  ½ *cup olive oil*
  3 *crushed cloves garlic*
    freshly ground pepper
    salt

To trim the artichokes, cut off the stem so that about 3 or 4 centimetres of stem remain attached to the head. Remove the hard outer leaves and, with a small, sharp knife, cut the top off the leaves to form a cone, then cut lengthways in two or in four, depending on the size of the artichokes.

Put the artichokes into a bowl of cold water, ice and lemon juice, and allow to soak for a couple of hours.

Remove the artichokes from the water, shake off as much water as possible, then dry with paper towel.

Heat the oil and add the garlic and, when the garlic is lightly browned, add the artichokes with enough stock to cover them. Season with salt and pepper, cover the saucepan, lower the heat and simmer until tender.

About five minutes before removing the artichokes from the heat, remove the lid and add the parsley. Stir well and serve hot.

Serves 4

Beans

I do not remember ever being served a dish of beans in Italy, other than at home. Even 'family dinner guests' were not served beans—it was just not the done thing. If one wished to eat beans when dining out, one had to eat at a trattoria where the speciality was 'Cucina Casalinga'—that is, home-cooked fare.

Green Beans with Cheese

INGREDIENTS:

    600 g stringless beans
    100 g grated pecorino cheese
      ½ cup olive oil
      2 tablespoons chopped fresh basil
      1 chopped onion
        freshly ground pepper
        salt

Cut off the tips from both ends of the beans, remove the strings, if there are any, but do not cut or break the beans.

Boil or steam the beans until al dente, drain, rinse under running cold water and set aside.

Heat the oil, add the onion and simmer on a low heat, frequently adding a spoonful of water, until the onion is ready to disintegrate. Add the beans and stir gently until the beans are coated with the onion and well heated.

Place the beans on a preheated serving dish, sprinkle the cheese and basil over the beans and serve.

Serves 6

Zia Emma's Beans

This recipe is a very simple way to prepare beans. The taste varies considerably according to what type of beans are used.

INGREDIENTS:

450 g white beans
3 tablespoons chopped parsley
½ cup olive oil
juice of 1 lemon
freshly ground pepper
salt

Boil the beans in salted water. When they are tender, heat the oil in a saucepan, drain the beans and put them into the hot oil as soon as you have drained them. Add the parsley and, for five to ten minutes, stir fry the beans on a brisk heat.

Remove the saucepan from the flame, sprinkle the beans with the lemon juice, taste for salt and pepper, stir, and serve hot.

Serves 6

Beans with Tomato

This is a delicious dish that improves every time it is reheated.

INGREDIENTS:

> 450 *g brown beans*
>   2 *cloves crushed garlic*
>   3 *tablespoons tomato paste*
>   ½ *teaspoon sage*
>   ½ *cup olive oil*
>   *freshly ground pepper*
>   *salt*

Boil the beans in salted water. When they are tender heat the oil in a saucepan, add the garlic and when the garlic is brown remove and discard it.

Drain the beans and add to the hot oil, stir until the beans are well coated with the oil then add the sage, salt and pepper and the tomato paste.

Stirring frequently, continue to simmer for about half an hour. Serve hot.

Serves 6

Green Beans with Vinegar

When I suggested that my mother-in-law serve the beans cold with simple salad dressing she agreed, and even liked the salad, but she remained convinced that green beans should only be served as a hot vegetable.

INGREDIENTS:

> 600 *g stringless beans*
>   ½ *cup olive oil*
>   ½ *cup vinegar*
>   *freshly ground pepper*
>   *salt*

Cut the tips from both ends of the beans and cut each bean into three or four pieces.

Put the beans into a small saucepan with a little water, oil, salt and pepper and simmer until the beans are tender, raise the flame, add the vinegar, stir and continue to cook briskly until the vinegar evaporates. Serve hot or cold.

Serves 6

Green Beans with Tomatoes

INGREDIENTS:

> 700 *g stringless beans*
> 500 *g peeled chopped tomatoes*
>   4 *tablespoons olive oil*
>   3 *tablespoons chopped parsley*
>   2 *crushed garlic cloves*
>   *freshly ground pepper*
>   *salt*

Cut the tops from the ends of the beans then cut the beans into 2–centimetre pieces.

Heat the oil in the saucepan, add the garlic and fry until it is light brown. Add the beans, tomatoes, parsley, salt and pepper, lower the heat, cover the saucepan and simmer until the beans are nearly cooked, remove the lid, raise the heat and cook briskly until the sauce thickens. Serve hot.

Serves 6

Red Bean Purée

The same purée, diluted with its own liquid, makes a delicious soup. Adding a piece of smoked beef to the beans whilst they are boiling changes the taste completely. The smoked beef can then be used as a meat dish or, chopped finely and added to the soup.

INGREDIENTS:

> 1 *kg kidney beans*
> 3 *tablespoons grated Parmesan cheese*
> 60 *g butter*
> 1 *onion*
> 1 *celery stalk*
> 1-2 *parsley stalks*
> 1 *carrot*
> *freshly ground pepper*
> *salt*

Soak the beans overnight.

Drain the beans and put them into a saucepan of water together with the onion, celery, parsley and carrot, bring to the boil, add salt and pepper and continue to boil slowly until the beans are very tender.

Drain the beans and vegetables and, in the food processor, purée all together. Put the purée into a mixing bowl, add the grated cheese, blend and taste for salt and pepper.

Pour the purée into an oiled baking dish, level the top of the purée with a wet knife and dot the top with butter. Bake, in a preheated oven at 350°F or 180°C, for half an hour.

Serve as soon as it is ready.

Serves 6

If you want to make the soup do not discard the water when you drain the beans and vegetables, but add enough of it to the purée to dilute it to the consistency you like.

For the soup, the butter and the cheese can be omitted.

Fried Green Beans

Fried beans are usually served after mixed fried fish or mixed grilled meat.

INGREDIENTS:

> *stringless beans*
> *olive oil*
> *flour*
> *freshly ground pepper*
> *salt*

Parboil or steam the beans until al dente. Drain and rinse under cold running water, spread on a kitchen towel and pat dry.

Toss the beans in seasoned flour and deep fry. Remove the beans from the frying pan with a slotted spoon. Spread them on paper towels and put them, covered, in the oven, at a low temperature, to rid them of any surplus oil and keep them hot until you are ready to serve.

Fried Cauliflower

To make the batter even crisper use flat beer instead of the water or stock.

INGREDIENTS:

> 1 *medium cauliflower*
> 1 *cup olive oil*
> *a little plain flour*
>
> *Batter:*
> 2 *eggs*
> 1 *white from a small egg*
> 115 *g flour*
> 7 *g baker's yeast or equivalent granulated yeast*
> ¼ *cup water or stock at room temperature*
> ½ *teaspoon olive oil*
> *pinch of salt*

To prepare the batter put the flour into a mixing bowl and form a well in the middle of the flour. Mix the yeast with the water or stock and add it to the flour together with the whole eggs, olive oil and salt. Beat with a wooden spoon until the mixture is homogenised. At this stage the batter should be quite thick. However, if the eggs are larger it may need a little more flour. Beat the egg white until stiff and fold it into the mixture.

Discard the leaves and break the cauliflower into florets. Cover the florets with flour, then dip each into the batter and fry in hot oil, turning it until it is golden brown. Fry only a few pieces at a time so that they are easy to control and do not break. Let the fried pieces drain on a rack in a warm oven until you are ready to serve.

Stuffed Cauliflower for Simchat Torah

I prefer to steam the stuffed cauliflower, rather than boil it. It is a lovely dish for a buffet or luncheon. It looks beautiful when served sitting in the middle of a round serving dish surrounded by steamed baby carrots, sprinkled with chopped parsley.

INGREDIENTS:

      1 *1kg cauliflower*
   400 *g finely minced yearling beef*
      1 *tablespoon chopped parsley*
      2 *tablespoons bread crumbs*
      1 *small chopped onion*
         stock
         freshly ground pepper
         salt

Ask the greengrocer for a cauliflower with most of its outer leaves. If they are damaged, remove them leaving the remaining leaves intact. Cut off the bottom of the core so that the cauliflower sits on its bottom without toppling over.

Put the cauliflower into salted boiling water and let it boil for about four to five minutes. Carefully drain the cauliflower without breaking it and, while it is still hot, gently push open the leaves without detaching them from the head.

Fry the onion in a little oil till light brown.

In a mixing bowl combine the minced meat with the bread crumbs, the fried onion, parsley, salt and pepper.

Distribute this mixture around the cauliflower, placing it at the bottom of each leaf, then close the leaves over the meat mixture and, with kitchen string, tie the leaves to the head so that the meat mixture remains in place.

Carefully place the cauliflower into a saucepan, cover with stock, and bring to the boil. Cover the saucepan, lower the heat, and continue to boil very slowly until tender.

The difficult part is not to overcook the cauliflower but to remove it from the water without breaking it. Place it on a serving dish and remove the string.

Serves 6

Braised Celery

INGREDIENTS:

1 *large celery*
1 *chopped onion*
3 *tablespoons chopped parsley*
2 *tablespoons tomato paste*
1 *cup stock*
½ *cup olive oil*
  freshly ground pepper
  salt

Remove all the leaves and any hard outer stalks, remove all strings then cut the stalks into 5 cm lengths.

Plunge the celery into boiling salted water, bring back to the boil, and continue to boil for three minutes and drain. If the celery is young and fresh boiling it can be omitted and the celery cooked directly in the tomato sauce.

Heat the oil in a saucepan, add the onion and fry until golden brown then add the tomato paste, stir and season with salt and pepper. Add the celery, mix well, add the stock, mix again, lower the heat and simmer slowly until the celery is tender.

If too much liquid is left when the celery is cooked, raise the heat a little and allow to cook uncovered until the moisture evaporates. Serve hot.

Celery with Tomatoes

This vegetable dish is also used as a very tasty sauce for macaroni.

It is also delicious when spooned over slices of left-over meat loaf, before reheating.

INGREDIENTS:

1 *kg celery*
500 *g ripe tomatoes*
2 *tablespoons tomato paste*
1 *tablespoon basil*
1 *tablespoon oregano*
½ *cup olive oil*
1 *crushed garlic clove*
  freshly ground pepper
  salt

Remove all the leaves and any hard outer stalks, then remove all strings and cut the stalks into 5 cm lengths. Boil the celery in salted water until tender, drain and set aside.

Peel and seed the tomatoes then cut them into small chunks.

In a saucepan heat the oil, add the garlic, and fry until it is brown, then discard it. Add the tomatoes, tomato paste, basil, oregano, salt and pepper and stir over a brisk flame for a few minutes then add the celery, cover the saucepan, lower the heat and continue to simmer until the celery is tender.

If the sauce is too liquid when the celery is ready, raise the heat and cook briskly, uncovered, until the liquid is absorbed.

Serve hot.

Baked Celery

Baked celery is a delicious luncheon or supper dish. It is also very practical because the celery can be prepared in advance, as well as the egg mixture, as long as you combine the two only when you are ready to put it into the oven.

INGREDIENTS:

1 kg celery
250 g Ricotta cheese
4 eggs
grated Parmesan cheese
olive oil
freshly ground pepper
salt

Remove all the leaves and any hard outer stalks, remove all strings then cut the stalks into 10cm lengths. Put the celery into boiling salted water and continue to boil until tender, drain and allow to cool.

In an oiled, ovenproof dish arrange the first layer of celery with the pieces lying next to each other, sprinkle lightly with grated Parmesan cheese and a little freshly ground pepper. Arrange the next layer with the celery pieces lying in the opposite direction, sprinkle with grated Parmesan. Continue until all the celery is used but, do not sprinkle cheese on the last layer of celery.

Mash the Ricotta cheese with a fork until smooth. Beat the eggs, season with salt and pepper to taste, but be careful with the salt because the Parmesan is salty. Add the eggs to the Ricotta, blend well and spread evenly over the celery and sprinkle the top generously with Parmesan.

Bake in a preheated oven at 350°F or 180°C, until golden brown. Serve directly from the oven to the table.

Grilled or Fried Eggplant

Nonna Rina said that eggplants drink oil. Of course she was right. When eggplant is fried it absorbs a large quantity of oil. That is why eggplant that is destined for the frying pan is always salted, left to stand for a while, then squeezed before it is cooked. This simple procedure changes the texture of the eggplant thus causing it to absorb considerably less oil as long as the oil is very hot before the eggplant is added.

This is a very versatile dish. As it has to be prepared in advance and because it tastes even better when allowed to rest in the fridge for a few days, it is often served with Sabbath meals. It is always served at room temperature, either as part of a cold antipasto, a summer vegetable dish, or as a salad with boiled meat or cold roasts.

INGREDIENTS:

> *use medium-sized, slender eggplants calculating*
> *approximately 1 eggplant for two people*
> *olive oil*
> *wine vinegar*
> *when possible use freshly chopped herbs, instead of the dry*
> *variety:*
> *mint*
> *parsley*
> *finely chopped garlic*
> *salt*
> *freshly ground pepper*

Slice the eggplant crosswise into slices about 8 mm thick.

Heat the oil in a large frying pan and when very hot add the eggplant slices. Fry until each slice is dark brown on both sides, or, if you prefer to grill the eggplant cut it the same way and grill under a hot grill coating the slices generously with oil several times whilst cooking.

Remove the fried slices from the oil and layer them on two or three layers of absorbent kitchen paper, repeating the alternate layers until all the eggplant is fried.

Arrange the fried slices side by side in a serving dish. Put the vinegar into a small bowl, dip your fingers into the vinegar and sprinkle it over the eggplant once only. Now sprinkle the layer with a generous pinch of parsley and mint and a little garlic. Repeat this operation until all the eggplant is layered, finishing with the herbs.

Serve at room temperature.

Grilled Eggplant

Eggplant slices are also delicious when cooked on the barbecue instead of the grill.

INGREDIENTS:

> 1 *eggplant per person*
> *lots of very finely chopped garlic and parsley*
> *olive oil*
> *freshly ground pepper*
> *salt*

Small, slender eggplants should be used for grilling. Slice the eggplant into 5-mm slices. Brush the slices with oil then grill them on or under a hot grill until they are well coloured on both sides.

Put the slices on a hot serving dish and sprinkle generously with garlic and parsley.

Eggplant Cutlets

INGREDIENTS:

> *eggplants*
> *eggs lightly beaten*
> *flour*
> *bread crumbs*

olive oil for frying
freshly ground pepper
salt

Peel the eggplant, then cut into slices about 5 mm thick. Coat each slice with flour then dip it into the beaten egg seasoned with salt and pepper, and finally coat it with bread crumbs.

Heat the oil in a frying pan and fry the eggplant until the slices are brown on both sides.

Serve hot, garnished with lemon slices.

Eggplant Alla Giudea

This dish is very popular and appears under this name even in the most luxurious restaurants all over Italy.

INGREDIENTS:

> 1.2 *kg eggplants*
> 3 *tablespoons chopped parsley*
> 3 *crushed cloves garlic*
> 4 *cups olive oil*
> *coarse salt*

For this dish choose eggplants that are slender. Cut the eggplants lengthways into four and then across into 2-centimetre-long pieces.

Put the eggplant into a colander and mix with a generous fistful of coarse salt, then cover with a plate, put a weight on top, and allow to stand for two hours. Rinse under cold water and squeeze dry.

In a saucepan heat the oil, add the garlic, a little parsley and the eggplant, cover the saucepan and cook on medium heat.

The trick is to remove the lid at the right time, i.e. when, touched with a fork the eggplant feels a little soft, at that point continue to fry uncovered, on a higher heat, until the eggplant is browned.

When ready remove the eggplant with a slotted spoon, place it on a preheated serving dish and sprinkle with the remaining parsley before serving. Serve hot.

Serves 6

Fishermen's Eggplant Salad

I don't really know whether this salad is popular with the fishermen or not but, as well as in the Jewish kitchen, it is the name under which I have usually found it listed on the menu in a bistro or a country taverna, in Italy.

INGREDIENTS:

     1 *kg eggplants*
     3 *quartered garlic cloves*
     ½ *cup vinegar*
     1 *hot red chilli*
     ½ *cup chopped parsley*
 4-5 *tablespoons olive oil*
       salt

Cut the eggplants into halves and boil in salted water until soft. Drain and cut into large chunks.

In a salad bowl combine vinegar, oil, garlic, chilli and salt, then add the eggplant and toss it until all the eggplant is well coated. Cover and refrigerate for 24 hours, during which time the eggplant should be tossed several times.

Before serving remove the eggplant from the marinade, pour a trickle of oil over it and sprinkle with parsley.

If you do not want to toss the eggplant while it is in the fridge, prepare enough marinade to cover all the eggplant.

Serves 4-6

Eggplant with Tomatoes

INGREDIENTS:

       1 *kg eggplants*
 1.200 *g peeled ripe tomatoes*
       1 *teaspoon dry basil*
       1 *teaspoon oregano*
       2 *tablespoons chopped parsley*
       2 *cups olive oil*

    2 crushed cloves garlic
    salt and pepper

Cut the eggplants lengthways into 1-centimetre thick slices and deep fry in very hot oil.

When the slices are dark brown, remove them from the oil and arrange them on paper towels, cover with another couple of layers of paper towels, pat dry, and set aside.

Cut the peeled tomatoes into small pieces and, in a wide, shallow saucepan heat three or four tablespoons of oil, add the garlic and remove it when lightly browned, then add the tomatoes, basil, oregano, salt and pepper, mix with a wooden spoon, and cook uncovered, on a medium flame, stirring occasionally, until the tomato juices evaporate and the sauce is concentrated.

Add the fried eggplant slices to the tomato sauce, bring to the boil and continue to cook on a low flame for five minutes.

Add the parsley and serve hot.

Serves 6

Nonna Rina's Eggplant

This dish is served hot or cold. It is worthwhile preparing it in advance and refrigerating it for a day or two. It can also be used as a sauce for pasta.

INGREDIENTS:

      1 kg ripe peeled tomatoes
      6 eggplant
  100 g pitted black olives
    50 g halved capers
     1 teaspoon dry basil
     1 tablespoon sugar
     2 tablespoons vinegar
     2 stalks chopped celery
     1 thinly sliced carrot
     1 chopped onion
     1 cup plain flour
     freshly ground pepper
     salt

Peel and dice the eggplant, put into a colander and mix with a generous handful of coarse salt, then cover with a plate, with a heavy weight on top, and allow to stand for two hours, rinse and squeeze dry.

Dust the eggplant with flour and fry in very hot oil until well browned, then drain on paper towels.

In a saucepan heat the oil, add the celery, onion, carrot, and basil, and fry until golden brown. Add the olives, capers, tomatoes, vinegar, sugar, a little salt and a lot of pepper.

Cover the saucepan, lower the heat and simmer until the sauce is thick. Add the fried eggplant to the sauce, lower the heat and continue to simmer, uncovered, for ten minutes.

Serves 6

Stuffed Eggplant

For this recipe choose eggplants of the same size, so that they cook at the same rate and look more attractive when ready.

INGREDIENTS:

    6 *medium eggplants*
200 *g minced veal or beef*
  ½ *teaspoon saffron*
  1 *teaspoon dry basil*
     or
  4 *chopped leaves of fresh basil*
  2 *crushed garlic cloves*
  1 *chopped onion*
     tomato sauce
  1 *cup olive oil*
     freshly ground pepper
     salt

Cut off the stem of the eggplant and discard it. Cut the eggplants in half, lengthways and, with a soup spoon, scoop out the pulp, leaving only about 1 centimetre of pulp attached to the skin.

Sprinkle the eggplant shells with salt and oil and set aside.

Chop the pulp with a knife, or put it in the food processor but be careful not to overdo it—you do not want a purée.

Heat a little oil in a shallow saucepan, add the onion and garlic and fry until both are golden brown, remove and discard the garlic, add the meat and chopped eggplant pulp and cook on a lively flame for ten minutes, stirring frequently with a wooden spoon.

Season with salt and pepper, add saffron and basil, mix well. Lower the heat and continue to cook slowly, stirring occasionally, for another 10 minutes or until the eggplant pulp disintegrates, and you have a homogenous mixture.

Oil the bottom of a wide oven dish and preheat the oven to a medium heat, 350°F or 180°C.

Fill the eggplant halves with the mixture and arrange in the baking dish side by side in one layer. Pour a trickle of oil over the eggplant filling, and bake for one hour.

Heat the tomato sauce and, before serving, pour a little tomato sauce over each eggplant.

Serves 6

Peas

INGREDIENTS:

> *650 g shelled peas*
> *4 tablespoons olive oil*
> *2 tablespoons chopped parsley*
> *1 small chopped onion*
> *2 cups water*
>   *freshly ground pepper*
>   *salt*

Put the peas, the onion, half of the parsley, oil, water, salt and pepper into a saucepan, bring to the boil, cover the saucepan and simmer very slowly until tender.

When the peas are ready, and all the water has evaporated, sprinkle with the remaining parsley and serve hot.

Serves 4

Peas and Lettuce

INGREDIENTS:

600 g shelled peas
   4 chopped spring onions
   3 tablespoons olive oil
   1 cos lettuce
    freshly ground pepper
    salt

Cut the lettuce leaves in half lengthways then across into strips about 1 centimetre wide.

Put all the ingredients into a saucepan and cover with water, bring to the boil, cover the saucepan, and simmer very slowly, stirring frequently, until tender.

When the peas are ready all the water should have evaporated.

Sprinkle with chopped parsley and serve hot.

Serves 4

Zia Lea's Peas

My sister-in-law Lea used to serve this dish when she entertained at dinner. It has a very delicate flavour and looks lovely.

INGREDIENTS:

650 g shelled peas
 30 g pine nuts
   6 tablespoons olive oil
   ½ cup dry white wine
   2 finely chopped onions
    salt

Put the pine nuts into a food processor with a little of the wine and work into a paste. This used to be done with a mortar and pestle.

Put the paste into a small mixing bowl and dilute it with the remaining wine.

In a saucepan heat the oil, add the peas and the onion and, stirring occasionally, fry until the onion is lightly coloured.

Season with salt to taste, add the wine with the pine nuts, bring to the boil, cover the saucepan, and simmer very slowly until the peas are tender.

If too much wine is left when the peas are ready, uncover and allow the wine to evaporate over a high heat. Serve hot.

Serves 6

Pea Pods

In Ferrara I was told that this dish is considered a delicacy, but in Rome I was assured that the same dish was called 'Pauper's Peas'—because one can prepare two dishes for the price of one.

Rich or poor, the dish should only be made in spring, when the pea pods are thick, tender and undamaged.

I have not given exact measures for the ingredients as it is very difficult to guess just how many clean pods will be obtained from any given quantity of peas.

INGREDIENTS:

> 1 *kg or more peas in the pod*
> *a little olive oil*
> 1 *clove garlic*
> *chopped parsley*
> *freshly ground pepper*
> *salt*

Shell at least one kilo of fresh peas and leave the shelled peas for another dish.

With the help of a small, blunt knife and a lot of patience, separate the outside of the pods from the inner lining, this lining is thin and nearly transparent.

The easiest way of doing this is to hold the pod with the inside facing you, then, either with the little blunt knife or just with your fingers, bend the upper tip of the pod towards you and gently pull the lining, together with the string, away from the outer pod and discard it.

Should the inner lining break during this operation, folding the pod at the breaking point will help you to continue.

When all the pods are prepared, wash them thoroughly, put the pods into a saucepan with a little water, some olive oil, lots of chopped parsley and a little garlic, season with salt. Bring to the boil, then lower the heat and simmer covered until the water has evaporated completely.

Sprinkle with vinegar and cook for another few minutes. Serve hot.

Fennel

When in season, fennel is widely used in Italy as a fruit, a salad vegetable or a cooked vegetable. When available choose long slender bulbs, although the larger round bulbs are just as good as far as taste is concerned and as long as the harder outer leaves are removed.

When fennel is used as a fruit it may be left whole or cut into wedges. It can be served on its own, or as part of a fruit or cheese platter.

When fennel is used for salads it is first cut into quarters lengthways, cored, and cut into strips crosswise. The width of the strips is decided by the cook's preference—I like to cut mine about 5 mm wide. Fennel salad can be dressed with wine vinegar, olive oil, salt and pepper, or any other salad dressing according to taste.

Fennel is also a versatile cooked vegetable.

Fennel in Tomato Sauce

INGREDIENTS:

> 6–8 *fennel bulbs*
> 6 *tablespoons olive oil*
> 1 *finely chopped onion*
> 1 *small tin tomato paste*
> 1 *cup beef stock or hot water*
> *freshly ground pepper*
> *salt*

Remove the outer leaves and cut the bulb into wedges.

Heat half of the oil in a saucepan, add the fennel and season with salt and pepper. Lower the flame, cover the saucepan and sauté slowly, for about 10–15 minutes, shaking the pan a few times.

In another saucepan heat the remaining oil. When the oil is hot add the tomato paste and dilute it with the stock. Bring to the boil and pour the sauce over the fennel.

Bring to the boil, cover the saucepan, lower the heat, and simmer until the sauce has thickened and the fennel is tender.

Serve hot.

Serves 6

Fennel with Besciamelle

INGREDIENTS:

> 6 *fennel bulbs*
> 2 *cups besciamelle sauce (see recipe page 214)*
> 1 *cup grated Parmesan*
> *salt*

Remove the outer leaves and cut the bulb into wedges.

Put the fennel into a wide saucepan placing the pieces next to each other forming only one layer. Add enough water to cover the fennel, season with salt, cover the saucepan and bring to the boil.

Lower the heat and simmer, covered, until the fennel is tender.

Preheat the oven at 350°F or 180°C.

Oil the bottom and the sides of an ovenproof serving dish. Using a slotted spoon, transfer the fennel into the serving dish forming one layer. Sprinkle the fennel with half of the Parmesan then pour the besciamelle over the cheese and sprinkle with more Parmesan.

If the serving dish is small, form several layers beginning with fennel and ending with cheese over besciamelle.

Bake until the top is golden brown and serve piping hot.

Serves 6

Fennel Alla Giudea

Cooking time for fennel varies greatly according to the season. When
the fennel is young and fresh use less water because the fennel should
be ready in ten minutes.

INGREDIENTS:

> 6 *fennel bulbs*
> 1 *crushed garlic clove*
> 5 *tablespoons olive oil*
> *chopped parsley*
> *freshly ground pepper*
> *salt*

Remove the thick outer leaves of the fennel, then wash, dry and cut
each fennel lengthways into four.

In a wide, shallow saucepan heat the oil, add the garlic and fry until
the garlic is brown, then discard it. Put the fennel into the hot oil, placing
the pieces next to each other forming only one layer, sprinkle with salt
and pepper, and add one glass of water.

Bring to the boil, cover the saucepan, lower the heat, and simmer
until the fennel is tender.

Transfer to a heated serving dish, sprinkle with parsley and serve
piping hot.

*Editor's note: Choose small fennel for this dish, or reduce the quantity
if only large bulbs are available.*

Serves 6

Lettuce with Anchovies

Cooked lettuce was a new experience for me. Before I came to live
in Italy I knew lettuce only as a fresh salad. I found that cooked lettuce
is very nice indeed, and so I have included a few ways of cooking
lettuce in this book.

If the lettuce heads are small, a whole head can be used per person.
When the lettuce is prepared it will appear to be too much to fit into

the saucepan, but as soon as the lettuce begins to cook the volume will be greatly reduced.

INGREDIENTS:

100 g pitted black olives chopped
50 g anchovy fillets cut finely
50 g capers
2 large lettuces
olive oil
freshly ground pepper
salt

Cut the lettuce heads in half, remove the core, wash the leaves and drain them well.

Beginning with the largest outer leaves, lay the leaves one on top of the other to reconstruct the lettuce shape, placing on each leaf a little of the anchovies, capers, olives, a little pepper and a trickle of oil.

Put a little oil into a wide saucepan then place the reconstructed lettuce halves next to each other, sprinkle with very little salt and a little oil, cover the saucepan and simmer for 20–25 minutes. Serve hot.

Editor's note: Cooked lettuce sounds unusual, but the practice goes back to ancient Roman times. A 16th-century Italian writer, Giacomo Castelvetro, describes grilled lettuce sprinkled with orange juice and says it is as good as asparagus.

Serves 4

Lettuce Frittata

INGREDIENTS:

400 g shredded lettuce
3 tablespoons olive oil
6 eggs
2 crustless slices stale bread
freshly ground pepper
salt

In a mixing bowl beat the eggs until they are frothy.

Dip the bread into water and squeeze dry, crumble and add it to the eggs together with the lettuce, salt and pepper and mix it all together.

Heat the oil in a wide frying pan, pour the egg mixture slowly into the frying pan, lower the flame and rotate the frying pan so that the eggs cook evenly all over.

When the surface of the eggs is set turn the omelette and brown the other side.

Serve immediately.

Serves 6

Endive Hearts

This recipe is a speciality from Rome, where it is known as Torzelli Romani.

INGREDIENTS:

> *1 head of endive per person*
> *olive oil*
> *freshly ground pepper*
> *salt*

If available, choose the smooth-leaved endive in preference to the curly type.

Remove all the green leaves, leaving only the yellow/white centre leaves or heart of the endive. Pare the core so that you remove only the superfluous part, leaving enough core attached to the hearts to keep them in one piece.

Bring to the boil a saucepan of salted water, add the endive hearts and boil slowly until the endive is al dente.

Remove from the water with a slotted spoon, carefully, so that the hearts do not disintegrate, lay the hearts onto a flat draining surface or a layer of paper towel and pat dry.

Heat about three fingers of oil in a frying pan and when the oil is very hot, fry the endive hearts briskly, a few at a time and always being careful to keep them whole.

Sprinkle with freshly ground pepper and serve piping hot.

Editor's note: The leafy greens we think of as salad vegetables, to be served raw, are often cooked, as in the lettuce recipes in this chapter.

Braised Cos Lettuce

INGREDIENTS:

> 6 *small cos lettuces*
> 100 *g goose fat*
> *or*
> *olive oil*
> 2 *cups stock*
> 2 *sliced carrots*
> 3 *sliced onions*
> *chopped parsley*
> *freshly ground pepper*
> *salt*

Wash the cos whole, without separating the leaves from the core.

Arrange the cos heads, lying on their sides, in a saucepan. Pour salted, boiling water over the lettuce heads, cover the saucepan and boil for 10 minutes.

Carefully remove the cos from the water, place it on a rack, rinse under cold water and drain.

Put the fat or oil into an ovenproof dish and arrange the carrots and onions in one layer. Make the following layer arranging the cos heads next to each other. Sprinkle with salt and pepper. Slowly, without disturbing the layers of the vegetables, pour the stock over the cos and sprinkle with the parsley.

Place the dish into the preheated oven and bake at 350°F or 180°C for 1 hour or until the liquid has evaporated. The longer the vegetables bake the tastier they become.

Serve hot.

Serves 4

Peperonata

INGREDIENTS:

> *1 kg peppers*
> *500 g ripe tomatoes*
> *½ cup olive oil*
> *5 tablespoons vinegar*
> *2 sliced onions*
> *freshly ground pepper*
> *salt*

Peel and seed the tomatoes and cut into chunks. Cut the peppers lengthways, into four, remove the core, seeds and pith, then slice crossways into strips.

Put the peppers, tomatoes, onions, oil, salt and pepper into a saucepan on a medium heat, cover the saucepan and, stirring occasionally, cook slowly for an hour.

Uncover, add the vinegar and cook briskly until the liquid has evaporated.

Serve hot or cold.

Serves 6

Stuffed Peppers

Sorting through several shoe-boxes full of recipes collected over the years, I found recipes scribbled on the backs of menus, invitations to lunches and dinners, theatre programmes, and other odds and ends that brought back old memories.

This recipe was written on an elaborate ship's menu. The menu was printed on the back of an invitation to supper on New Year's Eve 1950, during my trip on an Italian ship from Haifa to Venice.

I well remember the food served during that trip. After the strict rationing (zennah) in Israel, the abundance, variety and the attractive way that food was served on board ship, made an indelible impression on me. The stuffed peppers were baked with rosettes of mashed potatoes piped around each pepper. I remember even the tiny, fresh sprig of parsley that was stuck into the centre of each slice of baked cheese that covered the top of each pepper.

INGREDIENTS:

> 6 *green peppers*
> 200 *g mozzarella cheese*
> 1 *teaspoon basil*
> 4 *tablespoons olive oil*
> 2 *tablespoons bread crumbs*
> 1 *egg*
> 3 *eggplants*
> *freshly ground pepper*
> *salt*

Choose peppers that will stand upright without having their bottoms cut off. Cut off the top of each pepper, remove the core and pith, and set aside.

Peel the eggplants and cut into chunks. Cut the mozzarella into six thin slices.

Stir fry the eggplant in hot oil until it is tender. Drain off as much oil as you can and mash the eggplant with a fork. Add the egg, bread crumbs, basil, salt and pepper and mix well.

Fill each pepper with the eggplant mixture and cover with one slice of cheese. Sprinkle with freshly ground black pepper and bake, in a preheated oven at 350°F or 180°C, for 45 minutes.

Serves 6

Grilled Peppers

This salad can be prepared well in advance. It should be served after at least 24 hours, and it can be kept in a jar or plastic box in the fridge for a couple of weeks. However, if it is refrigerated it should be allowed to return to room temperature before serving. It is an ideal picnic dish.

INGREDIENTS:

> 1 *kg green peppers*
> 2 *tablespoons vinegar*
> 2 *thinly sliced cloves garlic*
> *olive oil*
> *freshly ground pepper*
> *salt*

Put the whole peppers under a medium grill, turn frequently until the skin is crisp.

Remove the skin, which should now come off very easily, remove the core and cut the peppers lengthways into strips about 3 centimetres wide.

Arrange the strips of peppers in layers, seasoning each layer with salt, pepper, garlic slices and a trickle of oil and vinegar. Allow the seasoned peppers to rest for a few hours before serving. Do not refrigerate until the next day.

N.B. The trick is to grill the peppers so that the skin burns but the flesh of the pepper does not.

This is easier to achieve with the thick variety of peppers and, it is even easier on the barbecue than under the grill.

Peperonata with Olives

A variation of this recipe is to omit the tomatoes, use green, red and yellow peppers if available, and fry until the peppers are as tender as you like them. Add the olives and capers to the peppers as soon as the garlic begins to fry.

INGREDIENTS:

> 1 *kg peppers, green or red or both*
> 425 *g tin tomato purée*
> 100 *g pitted black olives*
> 50 *g capers*
> ½ *cup olive oil*
> 3 *crushed cloves garlic*
> *freshly ground pepper*
> *salt*

Cut the peppers lengthways into four, remove the seeds, core and pith, then slice crossways into 6-mm strips. Heat the oil in a wide saucepan, add garlic and when the garlic is lightly coloured, add the peppers and toss until all the peppers are coated with oil.

Continue to stir fry for a few minutes, then add tomato purée, stir, bring to the boil, cover the saucepan and lower the heat. Stirring frequently, fry for 30 minutes.

Add the olives and capers, season with pepper and taste for salt;

because the olives and capers are very salty, additional salt is usually not necessary. Continue to cook covered for 10 minutes, then uncover and cook until tomato has thickened.

Serve hot or cold.

Zucchini

INGREDIENTS:

>   1 kg zucchini
>   2 tablespoons chopped parsley
>   ½ cup olive oil
>   1 onion chopped finely
>   freshly ground pepper
>   salt

Remove the ends of the zucchini and cut first lengthways into quarters then across to form chunks of about four centimetres.

Heat the oil, add the onion and fry until the onion is light brown. Add the zucchini, season with salt and pepper and, stirring frequently, continue to cook slowly until the zucchini are tender, but not overcooked.

Sprinkle with parsley and serve hot.

Zucchini in Vinegar

Nonna Rina made zucchini in vinegar using fresh mint leaves instead of the basil and parsley, but I like to use all three.

INGREDIENTS:

>   6 large zucchini
>   2 tablespoons chopped mint
>   ½ cup chopped fresh basil
>   1 bunch Italian parsley chopped
>   4–5 sliced cloves garlic
>   olive oil
>   vinegar
>   freshly ground pepper
>   salt

Cut the zucchini crossways into 6-millimetre-wide slices.

Heat enough oil to deep fry the zucchini slices until they are dark brown on both sides.

In an earthenware, glass or plastic container with a tightly fitting lid, arrange the fried slices of zucchini in layers, put a few pieces of garlic on each layer as well as a lot of parsley, a little basil and mint, salt and pepper.

Boil enough vinegar to cover the zucchini, pour it while hot over the zucchini and cover the jar.

Allow the zucchini to stand one or two days before serving.

Serve cold, on its own or as part of an assorted antipasto.

Nonna Rina's Zucchini

This dish is very popular in Torino. It should be served cold as a salad.

INGREDIENTS:

> 1 *kg small zucchini*
> 3 *tablespoons olive oil*
> 2 *tablespoons chopped parsley*
> 1 *cup vinegar*
> 3 *egg yolks*
> *freshly ground pepper*
> *salt*

In a mixing bowl blend the vinegar with the egg yolks, salt and pepper and set aside.

Cut the zucchini lengthways into four then across into halves.

Heat the oil, add the zucchini and parsley, and season with salt and pepper. Simmer slowly, adding one tablespoon of stock or water when necessary to avoid sticking, and stir frequently, until the zucchini are al dente, raise the heat to medium, stir the egg and vinegar mixture and pour it over the zucchini.

With a wooden spoon stir for a minute or two until the egg begins to curdle, then tip it onto a plate and allow it to cool.

Zucchini with Tuna

INGREDIENTS:

  1 kg peeled tomato chunks
 50 g rindless bread
185 g tin tuna in oil
  2 tablespoons chopped parsley
  3 tablespoons tomato paste
  ½ cup olive oil
  2 cups stock
  6 medium-sized zucchini
  2 crushed cloves garlic
    freshly ground pepper
    salt

Cut the zucchini in half lengthways and carefully scoop out the centre of the zucchini without breaking them.

Dip the bread in stock, squeeze dry and put it into a mixing bowl together with one tablespoon of oil. Mash the oil into the bread until it becomes a smooth paste. With a fork mash the tuna into a paste then add it to the bread, together with the parsley, salt and pepper and blend into a homogenised mixture.

Fill the zucchini with the mixture.

Heat the oil in a wide shallow ovenproof dish, large enough to accommodate all the zucchini in one layer, then add the garlic and fry until light brown. Add the tomato paste and peeled tomatoes and bring to the boil, the tomato sauce should nearly cover the zucchini.

Put the zucchini into the tomato sauce arranging them side by side to form one layer, bring to the boil, continue to boil for one minute then transfer the dish to the preheated oven and bake at 350°F or 180°C for one hour or until the zucchini are cooked without falling apart, serve hot.

Serves 4

Marrow and Pumpkin

For this, as well as all other pumpkin recipes, the pumpkin used is not the yellow pumpkin but the long, oval, light green pumpkin that is easily peeled and cored whole. However any variety of pumpkin can be used, even large zucchini.

Obviously, using yellow pumpkin instead of the green variety will give the dish a different colour, texture and taste.

Editor's note: The Italian word is zucca, which can translate to pumpkin, marrow or squash. It is popular among Italian Jews.

Sweet and Sour Pumpkin

INGREDIENTS:

> 500 *g pumpkin*
> 2 *cups olive oil*
> 1 *tablespoon sugar*
> 1 *teaspoon dry mint*
> *or*
> 3-4 *chopped fresh mint leaves*
> ½ *cup vinegar*
> 1 *clove chopped garlic*
> *freshly ground pepper*
> *salt*

Remove centre and peel the pumpkin, then cut into 5-mm slices.

Heat the oil in a wide, shallow saucepan and fry the pumpkin slices, a few at a time, until brown and tender. Drain on paper towels, and keep warm.

Remove most of the oil from the saucepan, reheat the remaining oil, return the pumpkin slices to the saucepan, combine the vinegar, mint, sugar, garlic, salt and pepper and sprinkle it over the pumpkin. Continue to cook slowly, turning the pumpkin slices over several times, for about ten minutes, or until tender.

Serve hot.

Editor's note: The sweet and sour flavours seem to be a characteristic of many Italian-Jewish recipes.

Fried Pumpkin Flowers

Pumpkin flowers are mostly used for cooking when they are still closed, although open flowers are just as good. The flowers are cut leaving about two centimetres of stalk attached.

Fried pumpkin flowers are often used as a dessert. If you want to do this, substitute two tablespoons of castor sugar for the salt, and before serving sprinkle with icing sugar.

Editor's note: Zucchini flowers are just as good, but the recipe is only worth making if you have an abundance of zucchini or marrow growing in the garden. Many of the recipes given here are ideal for those who grow their own zucchini in summer, especially since zucchini have a habit of growing from too small to too large within a day. If you are picking the flowers, pick them early in the day and handle them carefully because they are very fragile. Female flowers should be used for preference.

INGREDIENTS:

> 10 *pumpkin flowers*
> *olive oil*
>
> *Batter:*
> 6 *tablespoons plain flour*
> 1 *tablespoon olive oil*
> 2 *eggs*
> *salt*

To prepare the batter, break the eggs into a mixing bowl, add the oil and beat with a fork, then add the flour and a pinch of salt and continue to beat until there are no lumps left. If needed, add a little water but keep in mind that the batter should be thick.

Heat the oil in a frying pan, take one flower at a time and, holding it by the stem, dip it into the batter, then into the hot oil.

Allow the flower to brown on one side before turning it over to brown on the other side, avoid turning the flowers more than once because they break very easily.

When the flowers are brown on both sides remove them from the oil and lay them on paper towels to drain. Serve hot.

Serves 6

Pumpkin Purée

This recipe, from Ferrara, has two tablespoons of sugar, and no parsley but, if our yellow pumpkin is used it is so sweet that I prefer to omit the sugar. The recipe with parsley instead of the sugar is from Naples.

INGREDIENTS:

800 g pumpkin
1 cup olive oil
2-3 tablespoons chopped parsley
1 finely chopped onion
freshly ground pepper
salt

Peel the pumpkin and cut it into small chunks.

Heat the oil in a shallow saucepan, add the onion and fry until it is lightly browned then add half of the parsley, and the pumpkin. Season with salt and pepper, and continue to cook, covered, on medium heat, stirring frequently.

When the pumpkin is tender put it into a mixing bowl and, with a fork, mash until it has the consistency of a smooth purée.

Mix in the remaining parsley and serve hot.

Editor's note: A version of this is often served at the dinner following the conclusion of the Yom Kippur fast.

Serves 6

Mashed Baked Pumpkin

This is an old recipe from Padova. The dish is usually served at the dinner after the Yom Kippur Fast. The green variety of pumpkin is used for the preparation of this recipe.

INGREDIENTS:

800 g pumpkin
100 g citron, finely chopped
5 tablespoons olive oil

> 2 *onions, finely chopped*
> *freshly ground pepper*
> *salt*

Remove the centre and bake the pumpkin in a preheated oven at 350°F or 180°C. When the pumpkin is tender remove and discard the skin, then pass the pumpkin through a sieve or put it through the food processor, and set aside.

Heat the oil in a saucepan, add the onion and fry until golden brown, then add the chopped citron, a pinch of salt, and mix until well blended.

Return the pumpkin to the saucepan in which you have fried the onion, put it over a brisk flame and stir constantly until it becomes quite brown. Serve hot.

Serves 6

Fried Pumpkin Balls

Fried pumpkin balls are very effective when used to garnish other dishes, particularly if both green and yellow varieties of pumpkin are used (see recipe on page 118).

With a butter ball scoop make the balls from the pumpkin, and reserve the remaining pumpkin for later use.

Heat about two fingers of oil in a frying pan, add the pumpkin balls, turning them frequently so that they brown evenly all over.

Remove the pumpkin balls from the oil and place them on paper towels to drain.

Stewed Mushrooms

There are innumerable varieties of mushrooms growing wild in Italy, and so every Italian recipe for a mushroom dish specifies which variety is to be used. I have omitted these specifications for I do not even know the correct English names for the various species.

INGREDIENTS:

> 500 *g field mushrooms*
>   4 *tablespoons olive oil*
>   4 *tablespoons chopped parsley*
>   1 *finely chopped onion*
>   2 *finely chopped cloves garlic*
>   *freshly ground pepper*
>   *salt*

Choose small mushrooms and cut them into four or six wedges.

Heat the oil in the frying pan or in a shallow saucepan, add the onions and fry until the onions are light brown. Add the garlic and when the garlic takes on colour, add the mushrooms and half of the parsley. Continue to stir fry for 10 or 15 minutes. Season with salt and pepper, add the remaining parsley, stir and serve immediately on a preheated serving dish.

Serves 4

Grilled Stuffed Mushrooms

This is a very versatile dish, it is a lovely entrée, as well as a delicious luncheon dish.

INGREDIENTS:

> 6 *large field mushrooms*
> ½ *cup chopped parsley*
> 2 *tablespoons bread crumbs*
> 1 *small finely chopped onion*
> 1 *large egg*
>   *olive oil*
>   *freshly ground pepper*
>   *salt*

Choose large, open mushrooms of the same size, and clean as usual.

Heat the oil and fry the onion until light brown. When the onion is brown put it into a sieve to drain off most of the oil.

Remove the stalks from the mushrooms, leaving the caps intact, and set the caps aside. Chop the stalks finely, put into a mixing bowl, add the egg, parsley, bread crumbs and the fried onion, season with salt and pepper and mix until amalgamated.

Brush the grilling tray with a little oil, arrange the mushroom caps on the tray, combs up, and distribute the mixture putting on each cap as much as possible without allowing it to overflow. Grill under medium heat for 6–8 minutes, and serve as soon as the mushrooms are ready.

Serves 6

Stuffed Fried Mushrooms

This really is a rather special dish but it is not easy to prepare without help. The preparation of this dish is one of the many treasured memories I have of 'doing things together' with my mother-in-law.

When dinner was ready to be served, and everything was prepared for the frying of the mushrooms, Nonna Rina started 'Operation Mushrooms'. Nonna Rina filled and coated a mushroom and handed it to me, I fried the mushroom and put the fried mushroom into the oven to keep hot until it was served.

Many years have passed since then and I have had a lot of practice frying mushrooms on my own, but I have never fried a mushroom yet, without thinking of 'Operation Mushroom'.

INGREDIENTS:

    20 *mushrooms*
  200 *g lean minced veal*
    3 *tablespoons plain flour*
    3 *tablespoons chopped parsley*
    3 *eggs*
    1 *egg yolk*
        bread crumbs
        olive oil
        freshly ground pepper
        salt

Choose medium-sized, cultivated mushrooms and clean them as usual. Not everybody washes mushrooms but, if you do, remember to wipe them dry.

Remove the stalks from the mushrooms, leaving the caps intact, and set the caps aside. Chop the stalks finely.

Heat a little oil in a frying pan, add the meat and the chopped mushroom stalks and fry on a lively flame, stirring constantly, until all the meat is sealed. Drain and discard all the pan juices, put the mixture into a mixing bowl and set aside.

In another mixing bowl combine one egg and one egg yolk with the flour and a pinch of salt and beat with a wooden spoon until you have a smooth, very thick paste. Add this paste, the parsley and pepper to the meat mixture and blend it all together. The resulting mixture must be too thick to run; if it is not thick enough add more flour.

Preheat the oven to 350°F or 180°C, and prepare a rack covered with paper towel.

Lightly beat the remaining eggs, prepare the flour and the bread crumbs on separate plates, and heat the oil in the deep fryer.

Holding one mushroom cap in the palm of your hand, fill it with the mixture, cover with another cap, then, holding the two caps together so that they cannot separate, cover the caps first with flour, then dip them into the beaten eggs and cover with bread crumbs. Carefully put the caps into very hot oil, and even more carefully, remove them with a slotted spoon when they are browned. Arrange the fried mushrooms on the papered oven rack and keep hot until ready to serve.

Serves 6

Stuffed Tomatoes

INGREDIENTS:

>   6 *ripe tomatoes*
>   120 *g rice*
>   50 *g butter*
>   2 *tablespoons grated Parmesan cheese*
>   12 *strips of mozzarella cheese*
>   1 *chopped garlic clove*
>   *freshly ground pepper*
>   *salt*

Choose ripe tomatoes that are shaped so that they can stand with the stem side down. Cut the tomatoes in two leaving the bottom part larger than the top. Scoop out the seeds and juice. Sieve the juice so that no seeds are left.

Boil the rice in salt water stirring occasionally. When the rice is al dente remove it from the heat and drain. Add the butter to the hot rice and stir until well blended.

In a mixing bowl combine the rice and the tomato juice, garlic, Parmesan cheese, salt and pepper.

Stand the tomatoes on an oiled baking dish and fill the tomato shells with the rice mixture, then put two strips of mozzarella over the top of the rice. Cover each stuffed tomato with its top. Pour a little oil over the top, sprinkle with a pinch of salt and pepper and bake in a preheated oven, at 350°F or 180°C, for one hour. Serve hot or cold.

Baked Tomatoes

INGREDIENTS:

> 1.5 *kg ripe tomatoes*
> 1 *teaspoon oregano*
> 2 *large sliced onions*
> ½ *cup olive oil*
> 2 *chopped garlic cloves*
> *bread crumbs*
> *vinegar*
> *freshly ground pepper*
> *salt*

Peel and seed the tomatoes, then cut into thick slices or into chunks.

In an oiled ovenproof dish arrange the sliced onion forming one layer, sprinkle with half of the garlic, half of the oregano and a little salt and pepper. Arrange the second layer with the tomato slices. Sprinkle with the remaining seasoning, bread crumbs and a trickle of oil.

Bake for one hour at 350°F or 180°C. During the baking time sprinkle several times with a little vinegar slightly diluted with water.

Boiled Onions

When, in early 1944, I came to Bari, Italy, I found that onions, as well as most other food, were a luxury of the past, of that fairy tale 'before the war' past. It was then that I realised just how important the humble onion is in everyday cooking.

Several yeras after the war, when I returned to Italy and the availability of food was again taken for granted, I noticed that raw onion was never served at the table.

I am sorry that I did not take a photo of the expressions on the faces of the family the first time I served a fresh mixed salad! It took quite a long time until at least some members of the family accepted the fact that such things as green peppers, cucumbers, radishes, even celery and onions can be eaten raw.

Unlike other vegetables, boiled onions are often served with the meat, mostly with boiled beef.

INGREDIENTS:

> *white onions*
> *chopped parsley*
> *or*
> *oregano*
> *olive oil*
> *freshly ground pepper*
> *salt*

Choose medium or large onions of the same size. Remove the skins and the first outer leaves. Boil the onions in salted water for 20 minutes or more, depending on their size.

When the onions are cooked and well drained, cut them in half, lengthways, and arrange them on a heated serving dish, cut side up. Pour a thin trickle of oil over each onion half and sprinkle with either parsley or oregano, and some freshly ground pepper. Serve hot or cold. If the onions are served cold, sprinkle with vinegar.

Glazed Pickling Onions

INGREDIENTS:

> 500 g pickling onions
> 50 g sultanas
> 2 tablespoons castor sugar
> 1 tablespoon vinegar
> ½ cup olive oil
> marsala
> freshly ground pepper
> salt

Put the sultanas into a cup, cover with the marsala and let them soak.

Remove the onions' skin under running cold water, drain and dry with paper towels.

Heat the oil, add the onions and fry, shaking the saucepan frequently so that the onions become evenly coloured on all sides. Add the sugar, vinegar and the sultanas together with 1 tablespoon of the marsala in which they have soaked, and two tablespoons of water. Lower the heat to minimum, cover the saucepan, and continue to simmer, shaking the saucepan frequently, for about 1 hour.

The dish is ready when the onions are golden brown and the pan juices are practically caramelised.

Put the onions on a serving dish, pour the pan juices over the onions and allow to cool. Serve cold.

Serves 4

Pickling Onions in Wine

When, as a little boy, my son Ronald was asked what he had for dinner, he prompty answered: 'Drunk Onions!' Pickling onions do tend to roll around on an empty plate.

INGREDIENTS:

> 1 *kg pickling onions*
> 2 *tablespoons chopped parsley*
> 1 *teaspoon flour*
> 3 *cups dry white wine*
> ¾ *cup olive oil*
>   *salt*

Peel off the outer skin without bruising the onions and soak them in a bowl of cold water for 1 hour. After an hour, drain and dry with paper towel.

Heat the oil and, when hot, add the onions, season with a little salt and sprinkle with the flour. Very slowly, over low heat, frequently stirring with a wooden spoon, fry the onions for about 15 minutes. Raise the heat, add the wine and bring it to the boil, cover the saucepan, lower the heat and continue to simmer until the liquid has evaporated and condensed.

Put the onions on a preheated serving dish, pour the wine sauce over the onions and sprinkle with parsley. Serve hot.

Serves 6

Zia Lea's Potato Chips

'Chips' is yet another word that triggers my memory and conjures up the picture of my mother in the kitchen in Vela Luka.

The little steamer that visited our village twice a week was known as 'Our Ship' but it was really a ferry that serviced Korcula and other islands off the Adriatic coast. It was the only regular connection the island had with the mainland. It carried passengers and mail as well as our rations—salt and so-called flour.

Carabinieri, the Italian Military Police, travelled to and fro on 'Our Ship' and so did the islanders. The islanders received restricted travelling passes, unlike the Jewish refugees who were not allowed to leave the village.

As soon as a boat, any boat, appeared at the mouth of our little bay it was spotted by somebody in the village and the cry—boat! boat! was heard in the whole village. By the time the boat docked a curious crowd had gathered at the pier to see who was on board and what was being unloaded.

In our family there was a tacit law about meeting boats. Uncle, who always knew everything about the village and the villagers, met any floating object that attached itself to the pier; Aunty never met a boat because she considered the curiosity it implied lacking in dignity; Mama had always shunned crowds, so she never met a boat; Cousin Vera and I were allowed to meet the steamer, but not the trawlers, because Uncle had decreed the language used by the trawler crews unfitting for our young ears.

Because our very existence depended on the good-will of the carabinieri, it was very important indeed that Uncle should always meet the ship—it was the best way to keep informed about the comings and goings of the carabinieri officers.

Rations seldom arrived on the day they were due and, by meeting each ship, Uncle secured a place at the beginning of the queue that formed quickly when the voice spread that rations were on board.

Then there were the trawlers Uncle had to meet. Only very infrequently would an unscheduled trawler arrive bringing such unexpected bounties as rotten apples or rotten cabbages. Uncle, our *pater familias*, as well as the family's financial administrator, still had some bargaining power so that he could barter for a little extra of whatever it was the trawler had brought. Always a good businessman (we had the largest quantities of salt and rotten apples in the village), he bartered with the villagers, exchanging the foul merchandise for our greatest treasure— olive oil.

However, according to Uncle's bartering tales, his greatest achievement was when he obtained onions which were jealously hoarded and guarded for the pickling of fish for the winter.

Once a treasure-bearing trawler actually brought potatoes. That day Uncle triumphantly brought home four healthy, fresh potatoes.

Mama, the family chef, after giving due consideration to the matter, decided to make chips. Carefully she peeled and cut the potatoes into chips, as equal in size as she could make them. When all the chips were cut, Mama, a chip in each hand, put her hands behind her back and asked each of us to choose the hand we wanted. After she had distributed all the chips Mama fried each portion separately. When all the chips were ready we sat around the kitchen table and in silent concentration nibbled like mice, to make the six chips last as long as we could.

I included this recipe because, even though chips are not a particularly

Italian-Jewish food, the way my sister-in-law prepared chips is a very practical method of achieving really crisp chips that can be prepared in advance.

INGREDIENTS:

> *potatoes*
> *olive oil*
> *salt*

Peel the potatoes, rinse and cut into strips. Pat dry with a kitchen towel.

Heat the oil in a deep fryer, add the potatoes and fry very slowly over low heat. As soon as the potatoes begin to colour, lift out the frying basket and drain the potatoes.

Return the oil to the heat, raise the heat, and only when the oil is very hot put the drained chips back into the hot oil and fry until light brown. Repeat this operation once again allowing the chips to fry until they are golden brown—drain, serve and enjoy!

The last frying needs only a few minutes hence, after the first two steps are completed, the chips can be put aside, even refrigerated for a few hours, and finished when you are ready to serve. Never add salt before serving chips, or you will lose the crispness.

Baked Potatoes with Onions

If the potatoes are to be used with a milchig meal, use olive oil instead of chicken fat and add grated Parmesan cheese, and diced Mozzarella cheese between each layer, ending with onion and cheese.

INGREDIENTS:

> 1 *kg potatoes*
> 4-5 *sliced onions*
> ½ *cup goose or chicken fat*
> ½ *lemon, juice of*
> *freshly ground pepper*
> *salt*

Prepare a greased baking dish and preheat the oven to 350°F or 180°C.

Peel the potatoes, cut into slices about 7 mm thick and put into a bowl of cold water and lemon juice to soak.

In a frying pan heat the fat, add the onions and stirring frequently fry on a lively flame until the onions are browned.

Drain the potatoes and arrange the potatoes and the onions in the baking dish forming layers, beginning and ending with onions, and sprinkling every layer with salt, pepper and a trickle of the fat in which the onions were fried.

Bake covered for half an hour then uncover and continue to bake for another half hour or until the potatoes take on a golden brown colour. Serve hot.

Serves 6

Baked Potatoes with Tomatoes

This is a delicious way of cooking potatoes—it is practically a meal in itself, followed by a fresh side salad.

INGREDIENTS:

> 1 *kg potatoes*
> 1 *kg large ripe tomatoes*
> 3–4 *cloves garlic*
> ½ *bunch parsley*
> *olive oil*
> *freshly ground pepper*
> *salt*

Peel the potatoes and cut into 5-mm-thick slices. Chop the parsley and garlic very finely and mix with salt and pepper.

In an oiled ovenproof serving dish, beginning and ending with tomatoes, form layers alternating tomatoes and potatoes and sprinkling each layer liberally with the parsley and garlic mixture.

Bake for one hour in a preheated oven at 350°F or 180°C. The dish is ready to be served when all the liquid that has formed whilst baking, has evaporated.

Potatoes in Dressing Gowns

If the potatoes are to be served with a meat dish, prepare some chopped chives, one or two chopped anchovy fillets and chopped parsley mixed with a little olive oil, and serve this instead of the butter.

INGREDIENTS:

> *old potatoes*
> *butter*
> *salt*

Choose potatoes of the same shape and of a medium size, scrub and rinse without removing the skin.

Heat a large saucepan of salted water and when it boils add the potatoes, bring back to the boil and continue to boil briskly for ten minutes. Drain the potatoes and arrange them on the middle rack of an oven preheated to 400°F or 210°C. Bake for about an hour or until tender.

Serve hot with a side dish of butter.

Editor's note: The dressing gowns of the title refer to the skins of the potatoes.

Garlic Potatoes

This was one of Nonna Rina's favourite potato dishes. It is a very simple and easy way to cook potatoes but, like most potato dishes, it does not lend itself to reheating.

INGREDIENTS:

> *1 kg Pontiac potatoes*
> *½ cup olive oil*
> *4 chopped garlic cloves*
> *salt*

Peel the potatoes and cut them into even slices a little less than 1 cm thick.

In a wide, shallow saucepan heat the oil, add the potatoes, sprinkle with garlic, cover the saucepan and cook slowly on a very low heat for about 40 to 45 minutes. During the cooking time shake the saucepan frequently to prevent the potatoes sticking to the bottom of the saucepan.

The potatoes, mixed with the oil and garlic, can also be baked, slowly, until golden brown edges form and the potatoes are tender.

Either way the dish should be served hot.

Serves 6

Baked Mashed Potatoes

INGREDIENTS:

> 1 *kg old potatoes*
> 100 *g butter*
> 2 *cups grated Parmesan cheese*
> *milk*
> 4 *eggs*

Peel the potatoes and cut into chunks, put the potato chunks into a saucepan. Add a pinch of salt and enough milk to barely cover the potatoes and bring to the boil. Lower the heat and continue to boil very slowly, stirring frequently, until the potatoes disintegrate, and nearly all the milk is absorbed.

Put the potatoes into a mixing bowl and, whilst still hot, mash until smooth. Add the butter to the mashed potatoes and mix until well blended.

By now the mixture should be cold enough to add one egg at a time, blending each egg well into the mashed potatoes before adding the next one. When all the eggs are in the mixture, add the grated Parmesan and mix until well amalgamated.

Generously butter an ovenproof serving dish and preheat the oven to 350°F or 180°C.

Put the potato mixture into the prepared dish and bake for about an hour or unitl the mixture has doubled its volume and is golden brown on top.

Serve immediately. If left to cool, the potatoes will collapse and the texture will become rubbery.

Vegetable Pizza

This is a Roman recipe, and is known in Rome as Pizza alla Giudea.

Editor's note: The reason for the name is that the toppings on many pizzas are not kosher, but vegetables are quite kosher.

INGREDIENTS:

> *Dough:*
> 300 *g plain flour*
> 150 *g unsalted butter*
> 　1 *egg*
> 　　*salt*
>
> *Topping:*
> 　3 *large artichokes*
> 500 *g shelled peas*
> 250 *g finely chopped silverbeet or spinach*
> 　3 *tablespoons chopped parsley*
> 　1 *chopped onion*
> 　2 *eggs*
> ½ *cup olive oil*
> 　　*freshly ground pepper*
> 　　*salt*

With flour, egg, butter and a pinch of salt make a smooth ball of dough, cover it with a kitchen towel and let it rest.

Remove most of the stems and all the outer leaves of the artichokes, then cut off the hard tops of the leaves and slice finely.

Heat the oil in a saucepan, add the artichokes, silverbeet, peas, onion and parsley, and stir fry for five minutes. Add a little water, season with salt and pepper, lower the heat and cover the saucepan. Simmer until the vegetables are tender and all the water has evaporated. Remove from the heat and allow to cool.

Prepare a round baking dish dusted with flour and preheat the oven to 350°F or 180°C.

Cut the dough into two parts, making one part larger than the other, roll out the dough, and with the larger of the two sheets, line the bottom and sides of the baking dish.

Combine the vegetables with the whole eggs and pour the mixture over the pastry, cover with the other sheet of pastry and, with a fork make several rows of holes in the top pastry. Bake for 45 minutes and serve hot.

Spinach

Spinach, cooked as in this recipe, is served as a side dish. However, spinach is often used as a first course, in which case it is not chopped but the whole leaves are steamed until tender. It is usually served at room temperature, seasoned with salt and pepper and dressed with olive oil and chopped garlic, with or without lemon juice. Silverbeet, broccoli, chicory, endive and any other green leaf vegetables are often prepared and served the same way.

INGREDIENTS:

> 1.5 *kg fresh spinach*
> 1 *finely chopped onion*
> ½ *cup olive oil*
>   *freshly ground pepper*
>   *salt*

Steam or parboil the spinach in very little water, drain and squeeze dry. When the spinach has cooled chop it finely with a sharp knife.

Heat the oil in a saucepan, add the onion to the hot oil and fry until it is lightly browned. Increase the heat and add the chopped spinach, salt and pepper, mix it all together, cover the saucepan, lower the heat and continue to cook, stirring frequently, for 10–15 minutes.

Spinach Roll

INGREDIENTS:

Dough:
2 *eggs*
200 *g plain flour*

Filling:
1 *kg spinach*
150 *g unsalted butter*
300 *g ricotta cheese*
100 *g grated Parmesan cheese*
½ *tablespoon grated nutmeg*
freshly ground pepper
salt

With the eggs and the flour prepare the same pastry as you would for pasta (see page 20). Cover the pastry with a kitchen towel and let it rest.

Wash and chop the spinach and sauté it in the butter until it wilts. Lower the heat and continue to cook for 10 minutes. Remove from the heat and allow to cool.

In a mixing bowl work the ricotta with a fork until it becomes quite smooth or put the ricotta through the food processor, working with a plastic blade. Add the spinach and the Parmesan, salt and pepper and blend well.

Roll out the pastry so that it forms a rectangle. Spread the spinach mixture over the pastry sheet and, with the pastry, roll it into a long salami. Roll the salami into cheese cloth and firmly tie each end, and the middle, with kitchen string.

Put a large saucepan with salted water on the fire and, when the water boils, carefully put the salami into the boiling water. Bring it back to the boil, cover the saucepan, lower the heat and continue to boil slowly for 20 minutes.

Carefully lift the roll out of the water and lay it on a flat working surface. Remove the cloth and string. Cut the roll into slices, arranging them on a heated serving dish.

When ready to serve, sprinkle with melted butter and grated Parmesan cheese.

Serves 6

Baked Spinach

A simple variation that makes this recipe into a very tasty entrée is to arrange toasted bread slices in a shallow, oiled baking dish, spoon the mixture onto the toast, to make individual portions, then bake it.

INGREDIENTS:

>   1.5 kg spinach
>   60 g minced pine nuts
>   20 g chopped capers
>   25 g sultanas, optional
>   3 tablespoons chopped parsley
>   8 tablespoons olive oil
>   2 eggs
>   3 anchovy fillets
>   2 cloves chopped garlic
>   freshly ground pepper
>   salt

In a saucepan heat half of the oil, and when the oil is hot add the spinach, sprinkle with a little salt and cover the saucepan.

After a few minutes, when the spinach is reduced, remove the lid and stir the spinach, then cover again and continue to cook on a low heat until the spinach is tender.

Put the cooked spinach into a mixing bowl and let it cool.

In another saucepan heat the remaining oil, add the parsley, garlic, anchovies and capers and stir fry on a lively heat for 5 minutes, then add this mixture to the spinach, add the eggs and blend well. Arrange the mixture in an oiled, ovenproof serving dish and bake for 30 minutes at 350°F or 180°C.

Spinach Roots

This is a very old Venetian recipe. It was given to me by the Signora Margherita, (see the recipe for Luganega on page 115).

Signora Margherita explained that this recipe was, in the 'Good Old Days', served only by patrician families. It was an 'Upstairs–Downstairs' recipe, i.e. the spinach hearts were served upstairs and the discarded leaves downstairs!

My friend served the spinach hearts cold as a side salad, usually with a minced meat loaf or boiled meat, and used the remaining leaves for another meal.

INGREDIENTS:

> *You will need several kilos of spinach to have enough roots to make this dish*

Cut off the leaves of the spinach about 2–4 centimetres upwards from the root, taking care to leave attached and intact the tiny centre leaves, the heart of the spinach, then remove the outer leaves and stalks that surround the heart.

Carefully scrape the roots to remove any trace of soil, and wash in cold water, changing the water several times.

Put the clean spinach hearts into a saucepan with half a cup of olive oil, salt and pepper, cover with cold water and bring to the boil. Cover the saucepan and simmer slowly, stirring occasionally, until the roots are tender.

Remove the lid, allow all the water to evaporate, then sprinkle liberally with vinegar and continue to cook uncovered, over medium heat until the vinegar evaporates and the roots are coloured.

Cabbage Venetian Style

INGREDIENTS:

> *1 cabbage finely sliced*
> *2 onions finely sliced*
> *½ cup olive oil*
> *2 cups beef stock*
> *2 cloves garlic crushed and chopped*
> *freshly ground pepper*
> *salt*

In a saucepan heat the oil and add onion and fry until the onion is transparent. Add the garlic and continue to fry until both onion and garlic are golden brown. Add the cabbage and one cup of stock, cover, lower the heat and continue to cook very slowly, stirring occasionally, and adding a little stock when necessary.

Season with a little salt and a lot of freshly ground black pepper about halfway through the cooking time.

When ready, the cabbage should be reduced considerably, it should have a deep brown colour, and all the stock should have evaporated.

Serve hot.

Sweet and Sour Cabbage

INGREDIENTS:

    1 medium sized cabbage
    5 tablespoons olive oil
    1 teaspoon sugar
    ½ cup dry white wine
      or
    ¼ cup vinegar
    2 crushed garlic cloves
      freshly ground pepper
      salt

Discard the large outer leaves. Cut the cabbage in half, remove the core, and parboil the cabbage for about 5 minutes. Drain and cool.

When the cabbage is cold, cut the leaves crossways into noodle-like strips. If the centre is thick discard it.

Heat the oil in a saucepan, add the crushed garlic and fry. When the garlic is brown, discard it. Add the cabbage to the hot oil. Stir until all the cabbage is coated with oil. Add wine or vinegar, season with salt and pepper, cover the saucepan, lower the heat, and continue to simmer, stirring occasionally and if necessary adding a drop of water or stock, until tender.

Cabbage and Rice

This is what Nonna Rina called a 'very common' dish. Cabbage was never popular in the family, but rice and cabbage is a tasty and very filling dish, and because it is also an economical dish it was often prepared on the day the washerwoman came. Washerwomen, even in my mother's house in Zagreb, were given a hearty meal in the middle of the day.

INGREDIENTS:

> 500 g cabbage, sliced
> 200 g rice
> ½ cup olive oil
> 5 cups beef stock
> 1 finely sliced onion
> freshly ground pepper
> salt

Heat the oil in a large saucepan. When the oil is hot add the onion and fry until evenly browned. Add the cabbage and stir until all the cabbage is well coated. Cover, lower the flame and continue to cook for 10 to 15 minutes, stirring occasionally, until the cabbage has wilted.

Add the stock to the cabbage, cover, bring to the boil and cook slowly for half an hour.

Add the rice, stir well to avoid the rice clogging and sticking to the bottom of the saucepan, and continue to cook slowly, uncovered, for another 18 to 20 minutes.

Editor's note: This hearty soup is also known as Jota. I find it is a good idea to add a tablespoon of wine vinegar to the cabbage.

Serves 4

Sauces

Agresto

Agresto is also called Jewish vinegar. In some Italian Jewish homes Agresto is still used on festive occasions.

In Naples, at the family lunch that followed Michael's Brit Milah (circumcision), my mother-in-law used her last bottle of Agresto to prepare a dish of Tagliolini con la Bagna Brusca (see next recipe).

In Melbourne, I continued with the tradition and made a bottle of Agresto to be used for salad dressing, at the lunch that was given by our friends Sofi and Leo to celebrate Ron's Brit Milah.

I have not made Agresto since. Over the years, during my visits to Italy, I found that Agresto is still being made.

INGREDIENTS:

unripened white grapes

Put green, unripened grapes into a large mortar and beat with the pestle until you have a thin juice.

Put the juice into a saucepan and boil until it is reduced to one third of the volume.

When the juice is cold pour it into bottles, pour a few drops of oil into the bottle and, when the oil has settled on the surface, close the bottle hermetically and store for a week before using it.

Bagna Brusca or Salsa Agresta

A very old recipe, Bagna Brusca is still used in Venice as a condiment for tagliatelle.

INGREDIENTS:

> *1 egg*
> *1 egg yolk*
> *1 cup beef stock*
> *or*
> *for milk dishes use 1 cup of the water in which the noodles were boiled*
> *½ cup agresto (see previous recipe)*

Beat the egg and egg yolk in the blender, then slowly, continuing to mix by hand, add the soup and the Agresto.

Pour into a double boiler and, over a very low flame, continue to stir constantly until the sauce thickens but be very careful not to allow the sauce to boil, or it will curdle.

Editor's note: Agresto is not usually thought of as a specifically Jewish sauce. But these versions which use eggs almost certainly date back to the 15th century and must have come with those Jews who fled from Spain. The same sauce or dressing is sometimes known as Agristada among Sephardic Jews from Turkey and Greece. Agristada is the Judeo-Spanish term for a lemon and egg sauce.

Serves 6

Green Pepper Sauce

This sauce, hot or cold, is often served to camouflage left over or boiled meats. However, if you want to use the sauce hot, the meat should be reheated separately before the sauce is poured over it. The sauce is also used as a condiment for pasta.

INGREDIENTS:

> 500 *g green peppers*
> 1 *onion*
> 7 *tablespoons olive oil*
> 1 *tablespoon tomato paste*
> 1 *teaspoon sugar*
> 1 *teaspoon vinegar*
> 3 *sprigs parsley*
> 1 *garlic clove*
> *freshly ground pepper*
> *salt*

Choose the thick variety of peppers.

The peppers, parsley, garlic and onion should be very finely chopped. This can be done in the food processor.

Dilute the tomato paste with a few tablespoons of warm water.

Heat the oil in a saucepan, add the minced mixture, tomato paste, sugar, salt and pepper and stirring frequently, simmer over a medium flame for half an hour.

Add the vinegar and continue to cook until the sauce thickens.

Besciamelle Sauce
(Bechamel Sauce)

INGREDIENTS:

    60 g butter
     5 teaspoons plain flour
    ½ cup milk
      salt

The easiest way to make bechamel sauce is to melt the butter in a saucepan, remove the saucepan from the heat, throw in all the flour at once and mix until it becomes a smooth soft paste, and only then, stirring constantly, slowly add the milk and a pinch of salt.

When all the milk is mixed in, and there are no lumps, put the saucepan back over a very low heat and, continuing to stir constantly, bring the sauce to the boil.

Remove the saucepan from the flame as soon as the first bubbles appear and immediately add the flavouring of your choice, grated cheese, nutmeg, pepper, spices etc.

Mayonnaise

To prevent the mayonnaise from curdling, a very finely mashed slice of boiled potato can be added to the egg yolk, mixing it very thoroughly before adding the oil. But, however finely the potato is mashed, the mayonnaise looses the delicate smooth texture.

By the way, in Italy the mayonnaise does not curdle—the mayonnaise 'goes crazy'!

I have made mayonnaise for more years than I care to remember and it has only 'gone crazy' twice. Of course it only happened when I was asked to show a friend how to make mayonnaise without curdling.

However, if the mayonnaise does curdle, there is a simple way to restore sanity to a crazy mayonnaise:

Put one egg yolk into a clean, dry mixing bowl and repeat the process for the making of mayonnaise, using the crazy mayonnaise instead of oil. The result is perfect and only one egg yolk is lost.

INGREDIENTS:

    3 large egg yolks
    1 cup olive oil
  2-3 tablespoons lemon juice
      a little French mustard (optional)
      pinch of salt

All ingredients should be at room temperature. Put the egg yolks into a bowl of the blender and, using the slowest speed, mix the egg yolks for 30 seconds.

Without altering the speed add the oil, half a teaspoon at a time, and allow each teaspoon of oil to amalgamate before adding the next one. When the mixture begins to thicken add one tablespoon of oil at a time, and continue to allow each tablespoon of oil to amalgamate before adding the next one.

Continue this process until you have a very thick paste that is easily detached from the sides of the bowl.

Stop the blender and add the salt, mustard and lemon juice, and stir until the flavour is to your taste.

Makes 2 cups

Salsa Verde or Green Sauce

Salsa Verde is used with boiled meats, cold roasts and cold steamed fish. Always serve Salsa Verde in a separate dish, at room temperature.

INGREDIENTS:

    2 cups chopped Italian parsley
    ½ cup olive oil
    1 tablespoon vinegar
    6 anchovy fillets
  20 capers
    1 very small onion
    3 cloves garlic

Put all the parsley, anchovies, capers, onion and garlic into the food processor and chop finely, but without letting it become a paste. Add the oil and vinegar and mix well.

Store in a covered jar, not necessarily in the fridge, for a couple of days before use.

Nut Sauce

INGREDIENTS:

 4 *hard-boiled eggs*
 1 *cup chopped parsley*
 ¾ *cup olive oil*
 50 *g blanched almonds*
 50 *g pine nuts*
 15 *capers*
 20 *pitted olives*
 2 *slices stale white bread*
  freshly ground pepper

Put all the ingredients into the food processor and blend until the sauce is smooth and homogenised.

Very nice with cold meats and fish.

Beggar's Sauce

INGREDIENTS:

 1 *hard-boiled egg*
 1 *tablespoon vinegar*
 1 *tablespoon water*
 2 *tablespoons parsley*
 1 *large boiled potato*
 1 *slice stale bread*
  freshly ground pepper
  salt

The recipe, as it was given to me, instructs:

'Moisten the bread with clean water, then sharpen your best knife and chop all the ingredients as finely as you know how, put them into a bowl and with a wooden spoon mix until you have a paste'. Obviously a beggar does not have a food processor.

Editor's note: The bread must be squeezed dry before being mixed with the other ingredients.

Tuna Sauce

This is a lovely sauce for milk meals.

INGREDIENTS:

> 100 *g tin tuna in oil*
> 25 *g capers*
> 1 *cup olive oil*
> 1 *egg*
> 4 *anchovy fillets*
> *juice of half a lemon*

Put all ingredients into the food processor and process until you have a smooth sauce.

Mushroom Sauce

INGREDIENTS:

> 250 *g sliced mushrooms*
> 3 *tablespoons olive oil*
> 1 *teaspoon flour*
> 1 *small chopped onion*
> 1 *crushed clove garlic*
> *freshly ground pepper*
> *salt*

Heat the oil in a small saucepan and when the oil is hot add the onion and the garlic, fry until golden brown. Remove and discard the garlic, then add the mushrooms and fry over a lively flame for about 10 minutes.

Sprinkle the flour over the mushrooms, lower the flame to a minimum, season with salt and pepper, cover and simmer for another 10 minutes.

Mushroom sauce is usually served with meat but is also very nice with poached fish or boiled fish.

Sweets and Cakes

Bollo-o-Bollo

The same cake is called 'Bussola' (meaning compass) in Venice, and 'Buccellato' in Central Italy.

INGREDIENTS:

> 500 *g plain flour*
> 35 *g brewers (compressed) yeast*
> 5 *tablespoons olive oil*
> 5 *tablespoons castor sugar*
> 1 *tablespoon grated lemon rind*
> 1 *teaspoon aniseed essence*
> 3 *eggs*
> 1 *egg yolk*
> 50 *raisins or sultanas*

In a small bowl dissolve the yeast with a little lukewarm water, one teaspoon of the sugar and just enough flour to make a thin mixture. Cover the bowl and allow the mixture to rest in a warm place until the yeast has risen.

When the yeast is well risen and frothy, rinse a larger bowl with hot water and pour the yeast mixture into the warmed bowl. Add the 3 whole eggs, the remaining sugar, the oil, lemon rind and raisins, and about half of the remaining flour. Mix well with a large wooden spoon, until the pastry is smooth. Cover the bowl and let it stand in a warm place for about an hour or until it has risen to double its size.

Turn the dough out onto a well-floured working surface, add the remaining flour and knead until you have a pliable, smooth dough.

Form either two oval loaves or, if you prefer, one long sausage to form a ring with a large hole in the middle. Put the finished shape on a floured baking tray, cover first with a kitchen towel then with a light woollen cloth and allow to rest in a warm place, until it has nearly doubled its size.

Brush the loaves with the beaten egg yolk, and put the tray into the preheated oven. Bake at 420°F or 215°C for 5 minutes then reduce the oven heat to medium, 350°F or 180°C, and continue to bake until ready. It usually takes about 45 minutes.

Editor's note: Bollo is Spanish in origin. The word means ball or bun in Spanish, and the cake probably came with Spanish Jews, in the 15th century. Recipes for bollo appear, perhaps unexpectedly, in The Jewish Manual, *the first English-Jewish cookbook, published in England in 1846. There are recipes there for Bola Toliedo and Bola d'Hispaniola, both slightly richer than this, but recognisably the same basic recipe. The author of* The Jewish Manual *was almost certainly Lady Judith Montefiore, wife of Sir Moses, the great philanthropist who came from an old Sephardi family that had come from Spain to England via Italy. Perhaps the recipes came from his family. In any case, it is often eaten to break the Yom Kippur Fast, as well as at Succot.*

Shok

This recipe comes from Tripoli.

The Romans brought Jewish slaves to Tripoli at approximately the same time (BC) when they brought Jewish slaves to Italy. Between the first and the second World War, when Tripoli was an Italian colony, a large congregation of Jews was still living in Tripoli.

During the time of Italian colonisation, many Italian Jews worked and lived in Tripoli, too. When these Jews returned to Italy they brought with them many local recipes that had, over the centuries, become integrated in the Jewish tradition. Shok is a good example of these recipes.

Shok biscuits are baked at Shavuoth. The biscuits are strung on gaily coloured ribbons. On each ribbon are eight biscuits, each a different shape. Each shape represents a special good luck wish, and in each shape a small hole must be made for the ribbon. The shapes are always the same:

spectacles—to see only good things in life
ladder—to climb high in life
purse—to have lots of money
scissors—to cut off anything bad in life
wheel—to advance in life
clock—to tick happy hours
dove—to bring peace
hand—to give out gifts.

The ribbons with the biscuits are given to the children of the family as well as every child that visits the home, or is visited, during Shavuoth.

Prepare the same pastry as for the Bollo-o-Bollo, adding a little flour to make the pastry firmer. Roll the pastry until you have a sheet about 7 mm thick then, with the aid of a little imagination, prepare the following shapes: spectacles, ladder, purse, scissors, hand, dove, wheel and clock, and do not forget the hole for the ribbon. Arrange the shapes on a floured baking tray, cover with a kitchen towel and allow to rise a little but not enough to lose their shape. Bake in a preheated oven, at 400°F or 210°C, until golden brown. Allow the biscuits to cool before stringing them on the ribbons.

Focaccia con l'Uvetta

INGREDIENTS:

    300 g plain flour
    120 g castor sugar
    100 g seedless raisins
     50 g finely cut candied lemon or orange rind or a mixture
         of both
      4 tablespoons olive oil
      2 tablespoons grappa
        or
        brandy
      1 portion granulated yeast
        or
        powdered yeast
      3 eggs

Separate the eggs and work the egg yolks with the sugar until the mixture is fluffy and very light in colour. Set aside.

Mix the brandy into the egg yolk mixture then, a little at a time, add the fruit and the flour.

When the mixture is well amalgamated, beat the egg whites until stiff and fold the beaten egg white into the mixture.

Pour the mixture into an oiled baking tin and bake in a preheated oven at 350°F or 180°C for about 45 minutes.

Dictinobis or Ciambelle di Kippur

Ciambelle (doughnuts), are traditionally served with coffee to break the Yom Kippur fast. However, my mother-in-law served a very light sponge cake instead. Eaten on an empty stomach, freshly fried doughnuts can be rather indigestible.

INGREDIENTS:

        this quantity should be enough for 25 doughnuts

    350 g plain flour
    100 g castor sugar
     30 g bakers yeast

   ½ cup olive oil
   ½ teaspoon vanilla essence
   ½ teaspoon cinnamon
   2 eggs
      grated lemon rind
      olive oil

In a large bowl mix the yeast with about half of the flour and half a cup of lukewarm water, cover the bowl with a kitchen towel and a woollen cloth and allow to rest until it rises and becomes frothy.

Mix into the frothy yeast another half a cup of lukewarm water, then add the eggs, sugar, oil, vanilla, lemon rind and flour and knead until the dough is soft and smooth.

If you do not have a doughnut-making gadget, sprinkle flour onto the working surface, spread the dough, patting it with the palm of your hands until it is about 3 centimetres thick, then cut out the doughnuts with a large, round cutting shape and cut out the holes with a smaller one.

Heat the oil in a large, deep frying pan and fry the doughnuts, a few at a time, until they are golden brown on one side, then turn over and fry the other side; doughnuts should be turned only once during the frying and should have a light ring around the middle when they are ready.

Sprinkle the doughnuts liberally with sugar before serving, serve hot.

Editor's note: The name, which looks Latin, is puzzling. It is used only by Italian Jews for these doughnuts. If the word were Latin, it might mean 'of something said to us', which is just as puzzling.

Ginetti for Succot
Almond Sticks

INGREDIENTS:
   500 g plain flour
   250 g castor sugar
   300 g ground blanched almonds
     5 tablespoons olive oil
     1 teaspoon cinnamon
     1 teaspoon aniseed
     1 teaspoon grated lemon rind
     1 teaspoon vanilla essence
     5 eggs

Preheat the oven to 350°F or 180°C.

Mix together all the ingredients and knead until the dough is smooth.

Roll the dough until it is 30 mm thick then, with a sharp knife, cut into 50-mm-wide and 15-mm-long strips.

Arrange the strips on a floured baking tray and bake for 15 minutes, or until golden.

Editor's note: According to another source, these recipes keep well in an airtight container for at least eight days—which is the duration of Succot.

Precipizi

The finished Precipizi should resemble Torrone. The recipe was given to me by a very dear friend from Ancona, where Precipizi are traditionally served for Hanuckah.

INGREDIENTS:

> *for each egg use:*
> *1 tablespoon plain flour*
> *1 tablespoon castor sugar*
> *1 tablespoon olive oil*
> *1 tablespoon liquor of your choice*
> *honey*
> *extra olive oil*

Mix all the ingredients together until you have a smooth pastry, then form little balls, each the size of a walnut.

Heat the oil and fry the pastry balls until golden brown, remove and drain well on paper towels.

Prepare an oiled, heat resistant working surface.

In a saucepan heat enough honey to coat the balls. Put the fried balls into the hot honey and stir carefully until all the balls are covered, then pour the whole mass onto the oiled surface. Spread the mass so that the balls are tight against each other and they are not on top of each other. With an oiled knife cut into sticks about 30 mm wide and 60 to 80 mm long. As you cut, transfer each stick onto another oiled surface, leaving space between the sticks so that they do not stick to each other, and leave until the sticks are cold and hard.

Shavuot Biscuits

INGREDIENTS:

> 500 g plain flour
> 125 g castor sugar
> 2 cups water
> ½ cup olive oil
> pinch of salt

Work all the ingredients together, kneading well until you have a smooth pastry. Roll the pastry with a rolling pin until it is about 3 mm thick then, with a pastry cutter or a glass, cut out round shapes.

Arrange the shapes on a floured baking tray and bake in a preheated oven at 350°F or 180°C, until the biscuits are lightly coloured.

Remove the biscuits from the oven and allow them to cool before you sprinkle them liberally with castor sugar or powdered sugar.

Roman Diamonds

I was rather astonished when, during a visit to friends in Rome, I was offered diamond-shaped biscuits with the admonition to eat them with due reverence. I was told that for many generations the recipe has been entrusted by a 'Venerable Roman Matriarch' to her favourite daughter. On holidays, biscuits baked according to this recipe are still served in Jewish homes in Rome.

INGREDIENTS:

> 2 kg plain flour
> 500 g castor sugar
> 300 g pine nuts
> 300 g ground almonds
> 300 g finely chopped lemon rind
> 300 g sultanas
> 2 cups olive oil
> sweet white wine

Warm the oil to barely more than body temperature.

Rinse a large mixing bowl with very hot water, dry it and sieve the flour into it. Add the warm oil and with both hands mix the oil into the flour so that all the flour absorbs the oil. Add all the other ingredients and knead until a firm, smooth dough has formed.

Roll out the dough into a 6-mm thick pastry sheet. Cut the sheet into 70-mm diamond shapes and, with the blunt side of a large knife, make a series of indentations across each shape.

Arrange on a floured baking tin and bake in a preheated oven, at 350°F or 180°C, until golden brown.

Pan di Spagna

Pan di Spagna (Spanish Bread) is just a different name for sponge cake.

INGREDIENTS:

> 170 g castor sugar
> 170 g plain flour
>   6 eggs
>   grated lemon rind

Separate the eggs and whisk the egg yolks with the sugar until light and frothy. Slowly, and continuing to mix constantly, add the flour into the mixture. Stir until the mixture is well amalgamated.

Whip the egg whites until stiff and gently fold the whipped egg whites into the mixture.

Spoon the mixture into an oiled or paper-lined baking tin and bake at 350°F or 180°C for about 40–45 minutes.

Editor's note: Pan di Spagna crops up throughout Italian cooking, and is a light cake usually used as the basis for more elaborate desserts like cassata. The recipe may well have been brought to Italy by the Spanish, who ruled much of Italy in centuries past. It is a popular cake among Italian Jews.

Spun Eggs

Spun Eggs was originally a Spanish recipe that has become very popular in Italy, so I was told. However, in Italy Spun Eggs are always used to garnish the Mount Sinai cakes for Purim and Succot.

INGREDIENTS:

> *500 g castor sugar*
> *300 g water*
> * 6 large egg yolks*

Put a very fine sieve or a piece of cheese cloth over a small beaked container and strain the egg yolks to rid them of all skin and impurities, cover and set aside.

Twist a square of oilproof baking paper into a funnel with a tiny opening on the bottom, and keep it in shape with sellotape or use a pastry bag with a very fine nozzle.

In a double boiler, boil the sugar with the water for a few minutes. To test the syrup: dip a very fine slotted spoon into the syrup, then lift the spoon and blow on it until the syrup forms bubbles. If the bubbles drop off the spoon the syrup is ready.

Keep the syrup bubbling in the double boiler over very low heat. Hold the paper funnel so that one finger closes the bottom, and pour in a little of the egg yolk, lift it over the syrup, open the bottom and, moving your hand briskly, allow the egg yolk to pour onto the surface of the syrup, forming very thin vermicelli like noodles.

When the surface of the syrup is covered with noodles, push the noodles down into the syrup with the slotted spoon, and let the noodles boil for a minute before lifting them out with the same spoon. Drain the noodles in a very fine metal sieve.

Repeat this operation until all the yolks are used up. To prevent the syrup becoming too hot, sprinkle it with cold water.

Always prepare the spun eggs one day before they are to be served.

Preserved Figs

INGREDIENTS:

     1 kg figs
  300 g sugar
  1.2 cups water
    2 tablespoons rum
    1 lemon

Peel the lemon, discard the rind and pith and cut the lemon first into slices then into strips.

Choose only perfect figs and insert a strip of lemon into the little hole on the bottom of each fig.

Heat the water until it is warm enough to melt the sugar. Remove the water from the heat, add the sugar and stir until the sugar dissolves then pour it into the saucepan with the figs.

Place the figs in a saucepan, bottom down, so that they stand upright and are tightly packed next to each other, but not squashed. Add the water and the sugar and boil slowly until the syrup thickens a little.

Remove the saucepan from the flame and allow to cool for ten minutes then arrange the figs in a glass jar, pour the syrup over the figs and close the jar with an airtight lid.

Chestnut Roll

For several months in 1952/53 I lived in Maiori, a seaside resort on the Gulf of Salerno, about 100 km south of Naples along the old coastal road and considerably less by the mountain road. At the time our only transport was a motorcycle and on this, with Mickie between us, we rode to Naples every fortnight. We made a habit of stopping to stretch our legs when we reached the top of the mountain.

During these stops we were befriended by a family who lived in a dilapidated hut in the woods with, at the last count, eight children—and number nine on the way.

This family subsisted on what they could grow in a small clearing around the hut. The only cash they ever saw was during the chestnut season. The chestnuts that grow in those woods are the large variety called Marroni. The bigger children climbed the huge chestnuts and shook the branches, the little ones gathered the fallen fruit, and Dad walked several hours to the nearest town to sell the chestnuts. I believe that the Sacerdoti clan ate more chestnuts during our winter in Maiori than they ever had eaten before or since.

INGREDIENTS:

400 g chestnuts
150 g unsalted butter
100 g icing sugar
75 g cocoa
150 g lady fingers
4 tablespoons rum
grated chocolate

The easiest way I found to peel chestnuts is to cut into the shell, across the flat side of the chestnut, with a pointed sharp knife, and peel off the outer shell leaving the inner skin intact. Put the shelled chestnuts into a saucepan with enough cold water to cover them, add a pinch of salt and bring to the boil. Continue to boil over medium heat until the chestnuts are soft.

Check the chestnuts after about twenty minutes by piercing with the point of a knife, cooking time will vary with the size and freshness of the chestnuts. When they are soft, drain the chestnuts and leave them to cool, just enough to be able to hold them without burning your fingers, and peel off the remaining inner skin—the hotter they are the easier they are to peel.

Purée the chestnuts with a potato masher of the old-fashioned variety or by passing them through a fine sieve. The texture of the purée should be that of finely mashed potatoes but do not put the chestnuts into a blender or food processor with a metal blade.

Whisk the butter in the blender until it is light and frothy.

Sift together the cocoa with the sugar and add the mixture to the butter together with 2 tablespoons of rum.

Grind the lady fingers finely, practically into powder, and add this to the butter mixture and blend well. Add the chestnut purée and 1 tablespoon of rum, and blend until smooth.

Spread a sheet of aluminium foil on the working surface. Mix the remaining tablespoon of rum with a teaspoon of water and spread it over the foil. Form a salami with the finished chestnut mixture, place it on the foil and firmly roll the foil over the salami. Fold the ends so that they are sealed and refrigerate for at least 4 hours or overnight.

When you are ready to serve, remove the foil and put the roll on a serving dish, sprinkle the grated chocolate over the top and slice with a sharp knife dipping the knife into hot water after each slice.

Zia Sara's Pudding

INGREDIENTS:

> 60 g castor sugar
> 40 g ground almonds
> 20 g sultanas
> 3 tablespoons plain flour
> 6 eggs
> grated rind of one orange
> orange marmalade

Oil a torte baking tin with detachable sides, and sprinkle it with bread crumbs.

Separate the eggs and whisk the egg yolks until light and frothy then add the ground almonds, sultanas, flour and grated orange rind and stir with a wooden spoon until well blended.

Beat the egg whites until they form firm peaks then fold them into the egg yolk mixture.

Pour into the baking tin and bake in a preheated oven at 350°F or 180°C, for half an hour.

Remove the tin from the oven, spread the marmalade over the top of the pudding and return to the oven for another 10–15 minutes.

Serve hot or cold.

Bruscandole

In parts of Northern Italy, Bruscandole are served to break the fast after Yom Kippur.

INGREDIENTS:

> *sponge cake (see Pan di Spagna)*
> *sweet red dessert wine*
> *cloves*
> *cinnamon*
> *castor sugar*

Cut the sponge into thick slices and toast it in the oven at a low heat. Turn the slices over at least once and toast until the slices are very dry, then put the slices on paper towels to cool.

In a serving dish arrange the sponge slices into layers, sprinkling each layer first with enough wine to soak the slices, then with the spices.

Allow to stand for a few hours or overnight but do not refrigerate. Serve at room temperature.

Signora Margherita's Honey Cake

This recipe was ceremoniously given to me, in Venice, by the Signora Margherita of 'Luganega' fame (see recipe on page 115)

INGREDIENTS:

> *300 g plain flour*
> *50 g sultanas*
> *50 g chopped nuts*
> *4 tablespoons castor sugar*
> *2 tablespoons rum or brandy*
> *1 teaspoon cinnamon*
> *½ cup warm water*
> *1 cup honey*
> *½ cup olive oil*
> *2 eggs*
> *1 sachet granulated yeast*
> *grated rind of ½ lemon*
> *juice of ½ lemon*
> *8 cloves*

Oil a baking tin and line it with oiled paper.

Preheat the oven to 350°F or 180°C.

In a little saucepan melt the honey with the warm water. Put it over a low heat but do not allow it to boil. When the honey has melted add the yeast and stir until the yeast dissolves.

Put the flour into a mixing bowl and add all the ingredients, leaving the nuts and sultanas until last. Mix well with a large wooden spoon.

Put the mixture into the baking tin and bake for 45 minutes.

Editor's note: Purim is one of the most light-hearted of the Jewish holidays. It celebrates the triumph of the ancient Persian Jews over their enemy Haman, minister to the Persian King Ahasuerus. The Book of Esther, in which the story is related, is read at this time. Purim is a time of carnival, of feasting and masquerade and even of drinking. This is one of the few times in the Jewish year when drinking is encouraged. It is a time for giving charity, and of giving and exchanging edible (usually sweet) gifts. There is a wealth of cakes and biscuits for Purim, and the one common to all Jewish communities is called Haman's Ears, or Haman's Pockets. The name varies, as do the recipes (in Eastern Europe Haman's Pockets are yeast pastries filled with poppyseed). But the message is clear, whatever the recipe: everyone wants a piece out of the villainous Haman.

Haman's Ears

Haman's Ears can be served either sprinkled with sugar or dipped in melted sugar. If you choose the melted sugar roll the pastry a little thicker than you would if sprinkling with sugar.

INGREDIENTS:

1.   *½ cup olive oil*
     1 tablespoon castor sugar
     4 eggs
     as much plain flour as needed to make a smooth, pliable pastry
     2 tablespoons brandy
     pinch of salt
     or

2.   60 g castor sugar
       4 tablespoons olive oil
       4 tablespoons dry white wine
       4 eggs
          as much plain flour as needed to make a smooth, pliable pastry
          pinch of salt
          or
3. 300 g plain flour
       3 tablespoons castor sugar
       3 tablespoons olive oil
       3 tablespoons rum
       3 eggs
          grated lemon rind
          pinch of salt

Whichever recipe you choose: mix together all the ingredients and knead until the pastry is smooth and pliable.

With a rolling pin roll out the pastry into a thin sheet. Cut the sheet into either rectangles or triangles, and deep fry in hot olive oil until golden brown.

When you remove the rectangles from the oil, place them on paper towels to drain. When cold sprinkle liberally with icing sugar.

Brassadel

A Purim cake from Trieste.

INGREDIENTS:

      90 g cooking chocolate
      50 g chopped lime
       4 tablespoons plain flour
       3 tablespoons olive oil
       3 egg yolks
       ½ cup castor sugar
          juice of 1 large orange
          grated rind of 1 orange
          grated rind of 1 lemon

Break the chocolate into very small pieces.

In a bowl mix the oil with the egg yolks. Add the grated orange and lemon rind and chopped lime, mix and slowly, a little at a time, add the flour and stir until well amalgamated.

Lightly oil a working surface and spread the mixture over that surface to form a thin sheet. Spread the chocolate pieces and the sugar over the surface of the cake mixture, then roll to form a long salami.

Bake in a preheated oven, at 350°F or 180°C, until the top is golden. Unmould the cake and allow it to cool. When the cake is cold cut into finger-thick slices. Arrange the slices on the baking tin and bake for half an hour, sprinkling orange juice over the slices several times during the baking time.

Strufoli

Strufoli is a very old recipe. In Italy Strufoli are prepared for Purim. However, they are just as popular at Christmas when they are served all over Italy, although I believe that Sicily claims them as a local speciality.

INGREDIENTS:

> 2 *tablespoons olive oil*
> 2 *tablespoons castor sugar*
> 1 *egg*
> *as much plain flour as needed to make a pliable pastry*

Mix together all the ingredients and knead until the dough is smooth and pliable.

With a rolling pin roll out the pastry into a very thin sheet. Cut the pastry sheet into 2-cm × 30-cm strips. Make a loose knot with each strip and deep fry until golden brown.

Remove from the oil and drain on paper towel. When cold sprinkle liberally with icing sugar.

Orange Strufoli

INGREDIENTS:

300 g plain flour
   3 tablespoons castor sugar
   3 tablespoons olive oil
   3 tablespoons rum
   3 eggs
     grated orange rind
     extra castor sugar
     pinch of salt

Mix together the eggs, sugar, oil, flour, rum and salt and knead until the pastry is smooth and pliable. Roll out the pasty into a very thin sheet.

Mix the grated orange rind with sugar and sprinkle it all over the pastry sheet. Roll it up very tightly and, with a sharp knife, cut into 1-cm wide strips. When all the pastry is cut, open the strips into noodles and carefully slip one end of the strip over the other to form a loose loop.

Deep fry in hot oil until golden brown and drain on paper towels. When the strufoli have cooled completely sprinkle with powdered sugar.

Pignoccate

This traditional recipe for Purim is still very popular all over Italy.

INGREDIENTS:

500 g castor sugar
400 g pine nuts
 50 g finely chopped candied citron or lime
  ½ cup water

Put the sugar and the water into a saucepan and melt over a low flame until the sugar can be spun (test the temperature on a sugar thermometer, if possible) but do not allow the sugar to become coloured.

Add the pine nuts and candied lime to the melted sugar. Stir with a whisk until it comes to the boil. As soon as it boils remove it from the heat and continue to whisk until it cools.

With wet hands form little oblong shapes. Place each shape on a thin wafer or rice paper and dry for a day or more, before serving.

Zia Ulda's Marzipan

INGREDIENTS:

> 300 g blanched ground almonds
> 600 g icing sugar
> 3 drops bitter almond extract
> vanilla sugar
> or
> finely grated lemon rind
> pink or green food colouring
> liqueur of your choice

Put the ground almonds, a little at a time, into a mortar and beat until a homogenous oily paste forms. When all the almonds are ready add the sugar, a little liqueur and the colouring to the almond paste and, working with a wet hand, knead until well amalgamated.

Form little balls and flatten one part of each ball just enough so that it can sit on the flat side and look like a little hill. Garnish each hill with chopped dates or crushed nuts.

Editor's note: Marzipan is sometimes known as the bread of Mordechai during Purim. Mordechai was the uncle of Queen Esther, the wife of Ahasuerus, and he is one of the heroes of the story. Marzipan is particularly favoured by Sephardi Jews. In Italy, marzipan is also popular at Shavuot, the festival which celebrates the first harvest of Spring and which is, by tradition, the time at which God gave the Law to the Jewish people at Mount Sinai. Marzipan for Shavuot is often made into hill shapes to resemble Mount Sinai.

Marzipan Hills from Trieste ...

INGREDIENTS:

> 1 kg icing sugar
> 1 kg blanched finely ground almonds
> 2 egg whites
> 3 drops bitter almond essence
> pink food colouring

In a double boiler melt half of the sugar with a glass of water. Stir constantly until the sugar has melted. As soon as the sugar begins to melt, slowly add the almonds. Remove from the heat and pour into a mixing bowl, add the remaining sugar and colour and mix until well amalgamated.

With wet hands form little conical shapes.

Dip each shape into egg white then roll it in grated chocolate.

...from Venice

INGREDIENTS:

> *1 kg finely grated blanched almonds*
> *1.2 kg castor sugar*

In a small saucepan boil the sugar with a glass of water and when it begins to melt add the almonds and continue to stir until it forms a ball.

Tip the sugar onto an oiled working surface and with a large kitchen knife, working all around, lift and fold the sides of the sugar. Continue to fold the sugar ball until it becomes white.

Working with wet hands form little conical shapes.

Editor's note: Almonds are common in Italian desserts, cakes and biscuits. For Jews, almonds—especially when combined with raisins—are symbolic of good fortune.

Almond Ofelle

INGREDIENTS:

> *Pastry:*
> *500 g plain flour*
> *250 g goose or vegetable fat*
> *1 tablespoon olive oil*
> *2 eggs*
> *2 egg yolks*

Filling:
- 1250 g ground almonds
- 100 g castor sugar
- 100 g pine nuts
- 50 g sultanas
- 2 egg yolks
- a little rum

Filling: melt the sugar with a little water then add all the other ingredients and mix until well blended.

Pastry: in a mixing bowl, working with your hand, combine all the ingredients. Turn the mixture out onto working surface sprinkled with flour and continue to knead until the pastry is smooth and pliable.

Roll out the pastry with a rolling pin until you have a thin sheet. Cut out round shapes. Put a spoonful of filling on one half of each shape, cover with the other half and pinch the edges firmly shut. Sprinkle the tops with powdered sugar and bake, in a preheated oven at 350°F or 180°C, until golden brown.

Almond Salami

Alkermes is a very sweet red liquor that is often used for its colouring properties as well as for its taste. However, I prefer to use a little rum and add a little grated chocolate to add colour to the salami, instead of adding artificial colouring.

INGREDIENTS:
- 225 g ground almonds
- 500 g castor sugar
- 50 g finely chopped candied lime
- 150 g almond slivers
- 2 tablespoons grated lemon rind
- 1 teaspoon plain flour
- juice of ½ a lemon
- 1 egg white
- 1 measure alkermes
- extra grated chocolate

Put the almonds, sugar and flour into a frying pan and, over a low flame, stir the mixture until it is completely dry. Remove from the heat and transfer the mixture to a mixing bowl.

Beat the egg white until very stiff. Add the beaten egg white and all the other ingredients to the almond mixture and stir until well amalgamated.

Turn the mixture out onto an oiled working surface, knead with wet hands and form the shape of a salami. Roll the salami in the grated chocolate or cover it with a chocolate glaze.

Refrigerate for a day or more and slice before serving.

Almond Macaroons

INGREDIENTS:

> 100 g ground almonds
> 200 g castor sugar
>   2 egg whites
>   almond halves

Beat the egg whites until stiff, gradually adding the sugar. Fold the ground almonds into the beaten egg whites.

With wet hands form little balls the size of a walnut. Arrange the balls on a floured baking tray. Put half an almond on each ball, pushing the almond down gently to form a little depression.

Bake in a preheated oven, at 300°F or 150°C, until lightly coloured.

Zia Emma's Almond Macaroons

INGREDIENTS:

> 1.5 kg blanched ground almonds
>   1 kg castor sugar
> 1-2 teaspoons grated lemon rind
>   3 eggs
>   6 egg whites
>   vanilla essence
>   icing sugar

In a mixing bowl combine all the ingredients and mix until well amalgamated.

With wet hands form little balls, arrange the balls on a floured baking tray, and bake in a preheated oven, at 300°F or 150°C, until lightly coloured.

When ready, the macaroons should be cracked on top and soft inside.

When the macaroons have cooled sprinkle them with icing sugar.

Amaretti or Bitter-Sweet Macaroons

INGREDIENTS:

> 300 *g blanched ground almonds*
> 300 *g castor sugar*
> 24 *blanched ground bitter almonds*
>   1 *sachet vanilla sugar*
>   3 *egg whites (large eggs)*
>   *almonds for garnishing*

Mix the almonds and the bitter almonds so that the bitter almonds are evenly distributed through the sweet almonds.

Beat the egg whites and, adding the sugar gradually, continue to beat until the egg whites are stiff. Sprinkle the almonds over the egg white and gently fold in.

With the almond paste form little balls. Arrange the balls on a floured baking tray then press an almond into the centre of each macaroon.

Bake in a preheated oven, at 300°F or 150°C, for 8–10 minutes, or until the macaroons are lightly coloured.

Almond Torte

INGREDIENTS:

> 300 *g ground almonds*
> 300 *g castor sugar*
>   2 *teaspoons maraschino liqueur*

6 eggs
whipped cream
slivered almonds

Separate the eggs, whisk the egg yolks with the sugar until light and frothy. Add the almonds and the maraschino and blend until well amalgamated.

Whip the egg whites until stiff. Fold the beaten egg white into the egg yolk mixture. Spoon the mixture into an oiled baking tin and bake, at 350°F or 180°C, for 45 minutes.

When the cake has cooled, cut it evenly across the middle and take the top half off. Spread a little less than half of the whipped cream over the bottom half of the torte, cover with the top half and spread the remaining cream over the top and sides. Sprinkle the top with slivered almonds.

Zia Emma's Short Pastry

INGREDIENTS:

250 g plain flour
125 g unsalted butter
110 g castor sugar
  1 egg
  1 egg yolk

Crumble the butter and mix it with the flour. Put the mixture onto the working surface and make a well in the middle. Put all the other ingredients into the well and knead until you have a smooth pastry.

Always allow short pastry to rest for an hour in a cool place before using it.

For biscuits roll out the pastry into a 7–8-mm-thick sheet and cut out the biscuits in whatever shape you choose. Arrange the biscuits on a floured baking tray and bake in a preheated oven at 350°F or 180°C until lightly coloured and very crisp.

Zia Ulda's Apple Cake

INGREDIENTS:

> short pastry (see recipe on page 241)
> 1 cup cold milk
> ½ cup castor sugar
> 1 tablespoon castor sugar
> 1 tablespoon plain flour
> 1 egg
> 3-4 granny smith apples

Prepare the short pastry.

Whilst the pastry is resting prepare an oiled baking tray with removable sides, and preheat the oven to 350°F or 180°C.

Peel, core and thinly slice the apples then mix with half a cup of sugar.

Roll the pastry into a thick sheet just large enough to cover the inside of the baking tin. Place the rolled out pastry sheet onto the tin so that it covers the bottom and sides of the tin and overlaps the top ridge of the tin slightly.

Arrange the apples over the pastry.

In a mixing bowl beat the egg with the remaining sugar then stir in the flour and finally the milk. Mix until smooth and no lumps are present. Pour the egg mixture over the apples and quickly put it into the oven. Bake for 45 minutes. When ready, allow the cake to stand in the tin, for at least 15 minutes, before removing the sides and sliding the cake on to a serving plate.

This apple cake can be served hot or cold.

Ricotta Cake

INGREDIENTS:

> short pastry (see recipe on page 241)
> 400 g ricotta
> 50 g sultanas
> 50 g castor sugar

1   *tablespoon plain flour*
1   *tablespoon pine nuts*
    or
1   *tablespoon blanched almond slivers*
1   *tablespoon lemon juice*
¼   *teaspoon cinnamon*
1   *teaspoon grated lemon rind*
2   *eggs*
1   *egg yolk extra*

Prepare an oiled round baking tin with detachable sides.

With a rolling pin, roll out the pastry so that you can cut out a round shape large enough to line the baking tin.

Separate the eggs and whisk the egg yolks with the sugar until light and frothy. Put the ricotta through a sieve and add it to the egg mixture together with the flour, pine nuts, sultanas, cinnamon, lemon rind and juice. Mix until well blended.

Beat the egg whites until stiff. Fold the beaten egg whites into the mixture.

Put the cheese mixture into the pastry lined tin and with the strips of remaining pastry make a wide grid over the filling. Beat the extra egg yolk with a fork and brush it over the top of the pastry.

Bake in a preheated oven, at 350°F or 180°C, for about an hour.

Cassola

Cassola is a very old Roman recipe. When I cooked the baby lamb (see page 131) for our Roman friends they often asked me to prepare a Cassola for dessert.

When I was first given the recipe, I remarked that Cassola is just a sweet rice frittata. I should never have made that observation, although it is true enough. My innocent comment sparked off a long tirade about Roman versus Neapolitan food specialties.

INGREDIENTS:

    2 *cups rice*
    1 *lt milk*
  500 *g ricotta*
  300 *g castor sugar*
    5 *eggs*
      pinch of cinnamon
    3 *tablespoons olive oil for frying*

Boil the rice in the milk until tender and until the milk is absorbed. Stir frequently because the rice tends to stick to the bottom.

Whisk the whole eggs with the sugar, then add all the other ingredients, bar the oil, and mix until well amalgamated.

Put the oil into a wide frying pan and heat, twist the frying pan until you have a film of oil all over the bottom and the sides of the pan.

When the oil is very hot put the rice mixture into the frying pan and fry on a low flame, keeping the frying pan edge over the flame and frequently turning the frying pan around to allow the rice to fry evenly.

Cover the frying pan with a large upturned plate and tip over. Slide the frittata back into the pan, cooked side up, and continue to cook as before until both sides are lightly coloured and the middle well set.

Pesach

Editor's note: During Passover, the festival of freedom from slavery, it is forbidden to eat bread or leaven. We eat Matzot instead, an unleavened bread which is a reminder of the haste with which our forefathers left Egypt with Moses.

Passover cakes are a genre of their own in cookery. They cannot be made with flour or any leavening agent, but where there are eggs and ground matzot (known as matzot meal), there will be cakes. Every Jewish household goes through dozens and dozens of eggs during Passover, and most of them are used in baking. This is a time when families and friends get together, and so there are always cakes and biscuits in the house.

Harosset

Harosset is one of the five symbolic foods on the Seder plate during Passover. It represents the mortar used in building by our forefathers when they were slaves in Egypt.

The preparing of the Harosset is traditional, hence it varies from one country to another, from region to region.

Because I believe them to be of interest, I include recipes for the making of Harosset (see Pesach on page 11) that I have collected, with the help of friends and relatives, from various parts of the world. I have always, even when I lived in Italy, prepared Harosset the same way my mother, Nonna, used to prepare it.

Editor's note: The sweetness of harosset is always a subject of much discussion in our family. We are always struck by the fact that a food representing something so painful is so delicious, and regard it as one of the rewards of past suffering. It is more likely that its sweetness is meant to allay the bitterness of the maror (bitter herbs); at a festival where children are so involved, that would be necessary. But it may also suggest that even the bitterness of slavery had its blessings in the fruit and nuts that the children of Israel would have enjoyed again when they regained their ancient land.

Harosset... from Zia Ulda, Padova (Italy)

INGREDIENTS:

>   150 g dry chestnuts
>   250 g peeled and cored apples
>   100 g blanched almonds
>   100 g pitted dates
>   100 g pitted prunes
>   100 g sultanas
>   1 teaspoon cinnamon
>   juice of 2 oranges

Boil the chestnuts in water, with a pinch of salt, until they are quite soft.

Drain the chestnuts. Mince the chestnuts, almonds, dates, prunes and sultanas in a fine meat mincer and grate the apples.

Combine all the ingredients and mix until well amalgamated.

... from Milano (Italy)

INGREDIENTS:

    1 *kg pitted dates*
    1 *kg ground almonds*
  500 *g peeled, cored and diced apples*
  500 *g peeled, cored and diced pears*
  250 *g castor sugar*
      grated rind of one orange
    3 *bananas*

Put the apples and pears into a saucepan, add water and boil until the fruit disintegrates.

Add the almonds, dates, and sugar and continue to simmer, over a low heat, for one hour. Add the peeled and cut bananas and continue to cook for one more hour.

Remove from the flame and allow to cool before adding the cinnamon.

... from Zia Emma, Napoli (Italy)

INGREDIENTS:

  250 *g ground almonds*
  250 *g dry chestnuts*
  150 *g ground pine nuts*
   50 *g finely chopped candied citron*
   50 *g finely chopped candied orange peel*
      juice of 2 oranges

Mix all the dry ingredients together, add the orange juice a little at a time, and mix until you have a thick paste.

... from Ancona (Italy)

INGREDIENTS:

  500 *g pitted, finely chopped dates*
  200 *g ground almonds*

   60 g finely chopped sultanas
    2 grated apples
     juice of 2 oranges

Combine all the ingredients and mix thoroughly.

... from Mama, Zagreb (Yugoslavia)

INGREDIENTS:

  500 g ground walnuts
  150 g castor sugar
    2 peeled and cored apples
    2 measures rum

Grate the apples on a fine grater, add all the other ingredients and mix until well amalgamated.

Editor's note: Mama Olga's harosset is closest to that prepared by my family, which is originally from Poland. We use a mixture of chopped walnuts and grated apples, flavoured with cinnamon, and moistened into a paste with sweet Passover wine. No sugar, however, because the apples and wine provide enough sweetness.

... from Sarajevo (Yugoslavia)

INGREDIENTS:

  200 g ground almonds
  500 g peeled, cored, grated apples
    ½ cup sweet wine
    2 tablespoons honey

Dilute the honey with the wine, mix the almonds and apples together then add the diluted honey, a little at a time, until you have a thick paste.

The quantity of honey and wine varies according to the juiciness of the apples.

... from Tante Mila, Vienna (Austria)

INGREDIENTS:

    350 g ground walnuts
    100 g minced sultanas
    100 g pitted, minced dates
     50 g grated cooking chocolate
    100 g castor sugar
        brandy

Mix together all the dry ingredients and add as much brandy as necessary to bind the mixture into a thick, homogenous paste.

... from Tel Aviv (Israel)

INGREDIENTS:

    20 pitted dates
     2 peeled, grated apples
     6 peeled bananas
       juice and grated rind of 1 orange and 1 lemon
     1 cup sweet wine
       a little coarse matzot meal

Chop the dates very finely, add the grated apples, orange and lemon rind, orange and lemon juice and mix well. Add as much matzot meal as needed until you have a thick homogenous paste.

... from Addis Ababa (Ethiopia)

INGREDIENTS:

     60 g pine nuts
    100 g ground walnuts
    100 g ground alonds
    100 g castor sugar
     ½ teaspoon cinnamon

    1 *mashed banana*
    1 *egg yolk*
       juice of 1 lemon
       grated rind of 1 lemon

Combine all ingredients, bar the pine nuts. Shape the harosset into a mound and stick the pine nuts, vertically, into the harosset to make it look like a hedgehog.

... from San'a (Yemen)

INGREDIENTS:

    500 *g grated apples*
    100 *g pitted, minced dates*
    100 *g minced dry figs*
     50 *g castor sugar*
     ½ *teaspoon black pepper*
     1 *teaspoon finely chopped ginger*

Mix together all the ingredients. If too dry add a little wine.

Chocolate Pesach Torte

INGREDIENTS:

    250 *g castor sugar*
    200 *g grated cooking chocolate*
    250 *g blanched ground almonds*
      8 *egg whites*

Beat the egg whites until they begin to stiffen then slowly add the sugar whilst continuing to beat the egg whites until very stiff. Gently fold the chocolate and the almonds into the beaten egg whites.

Spoon the mixture into an oiled torte baking tin and bake in a preheated oven at 350°F or 180°C.

Serve filled and covered with whipped cream, if desired.

Zia Emma's Almond Torte

INGREDIENTS:

    300 g castor sugar
    300 g grated almonds
      2 tablespoons maraschino liqueur
      6 eggs

Separate the eggs and whisk the yolks with the sugar until light and frothy. Add the almonds, matzot meal and maraschino. Blend until well amalgamated.

Beat the egg whites until very stiff. Fold the beaten egg whites into the egg yolk mixture.

Spoon the mixture into an oiled torte tin and bake, at 350°F or 180°C, for 45 minutes.

Serve filled and covered with whipped cream, if desired.

Zia Lea's Pesach Torte

INGREDIENTS:

     65 g fine matzot meal
    125 g castor sugar
    125 g ground almonds
      8 eggs
         grated orange and lemon rind

Separate the eggs and whisk the yolks with the sugar until light and frothy, then add the matzot meal, the almonds and the lemon rind.

Beat the egg whites until very stiff. Fold the beaten egg whites into the egg yolk mixture.

Spoon the mixture into an oiled torte tin and bake at 350°F or 180°C, for about 30–40 minutes.

Served filled and covered with whipped cream.

Zia Gioia's Pesach Torte

My first Seder in Napoli, in 1952, was at my sister-in-law (Zia) Emma's home. It was a memorable Seder for me in many ways.

It was the first Seder I attended since 1938 in Zagreb. There were numerous Sacerdoti and Levi relatives around the Seder table. Amos and I were the centre of attention because a. we had just arrived from Israel, b. I was the latest addition to the Sacerdoti family, c. I was not Italian but d. I did make up for that lack of consideration by being pregnant.

Gioia Levi's Pesach cake is the other vivid memory of that feast. It is my favourite Pesach cake and I still bake it every year. It is a torte, but it is so large that I always bake it in a large square roasting dish which I use for nothing else.

INGREDIENTS:

> 10 *large eggs*
> 7 *heaped tablespoons coarse matzot meal*
> 10 *tablespoons castor sugar*
> 400 *g freshly blanched ground almonds*
>   *grated rind of 1 lemon*

Separate the eggs and whisk the egg yolks with the sugar until very light and frothy. Add the matzot meal and the lemon rind and mix until it is evenly distributed through the mixture.

Beat the egg whites until stiff. Tip the egg whites onto the egg yolk mixture, sprinkle the almonds on top of the egg whites and with a large, wide wooden spoon, gently fold until well amalgamated.

Spoon the cake mixture into an oiled baking tin well sprinkled with coarse matzot meal. Bake in a preheated oven, at 350°F or 180°C, for 45 minutes. Serve with cream whipped with sugar and vanilla sugar.

Roasted Almond Torte

INGREDIENTS:

      8 *egg whites*
  300 *g roasted almonds*
  300 *g castor sugar*
  100 *g cooking chocolate*

Prepare an oiled torte baking tin, well covered with coarse matzot meal.

Blanch the almonds, pat dry, spread on a baking tray and put into a hot oven, shaking and turning the almonds frequently, until they begin to colour. Remove the almonds from the oven tray as soon as the colour is right. Left on the tray the almonds will continue to darken.

When the almonds have cooled put them into the food processor, together with the sugar and the chocolate, and grind until all the ingredients are reduced to powder.

Beat the egg whites until very stiff peaks form, then sprinkle the powdered ingredients over the beaten egg white and fold until well amalgamated.

Spoon into a baking tin and bake in a preheated oven, at 350°F or 180°C, for half an hour. Serve with whipped cream or zabaglione.

Zabaglione

INGREDIENTS:

  120 *g castor sugar*
   18 *tablespoons marsala*
    6 *egg yolks*

Whisk the eggs with the sugar, until they are practically white.

Gently mix the marsala into the egg yolk mixture. Spoon the mixture into a double boiler and, constantly stirring over a low heat, allow it to thicken but not to boil. If the mixture boils it will curdle immediately.

Zabaglione can be served hot or cold.

Zuccherini

During Pesach, Zuccherini are ever present in every Jewish home in Italy. I include recipes for Zuccherini from four different parts of Italy.

... from Piemonte

INGREDIENTS:

> 650 g fine matzot meal
> 300 g castor sugar
>   1 cup olive oil
>   6 eggs
>   cinnamon or grated lemon rind

Separate the eggs and beat the egg whites until very stiff. Add the egg yolks, one at a time, to the beaten egg whites, amalgamating each egg yolk as you add it.

When all the egg yolks are well amalgamated, add the oil and the matzot meal. Leaving the mixture in the bowl, knead until very firm and smooth.

With oiled hands form biscuit-sized shapes. Arrange the shapes on an oiled oven tray and bake in a moderate oven until very lightly coloured.

... from Verona

INGREDIENTS:

> 200 g castor sugar
> 500 g fine matzot meal
> 20 g aniseed
>   1 tablespoon olive oil
>   3 eggs
>   grated lemon rind

Whisk the whole eggs with the sugar until very smooth. Add the oil, aniseed and lemon rind and amalgamate well. Add the matzot meal very slowly, mix well, cover, and allow to rest for one hour.

With oiled hands form little S shapes and arrange the shapes on an oiled oven tray.

Bake in a moderate oven for 10 minutes or until light brown.

... from Padova

INGREDIENTS:

> 650 g fine matzot meal
>   5 tablespoons castor sugar
> 10 tablespoons olive oil
>   5 eggs
>   aniseed or lemon rind

Work as for the zuccherini from Verona.

... from Ferrara

INGREDIENTS:

> 15 tablespoons castor sugar
> 7 tablespoons olive oil
> 7 tablespoons chicken fat
>   or
> 15 tablespoons olive oil
> 10 egg yolks
> 5 egg whites
>   fine matzot meal

Whisk the egg yolks with the sugar until light and frothy.

Beat the egg whites until stiff. Gently fold the beaten egg whites into the egg yolk mixture.

Add enough fine matzot meal until the mixture is firm enough to make little shapes with oiled hands. Arrange the shapes on an oiled oven tray, and bake for 10 minutes or until lightly browned.

Scodelline

This is a very popular Italian dessert for Pesach. I received this recipe in Venice, in 1952, from the grandmother of a very dear friend. The old lady was touched when I told her that to begin my collection of recipes, I had copied my mother's recipes during my last visit to Zagreb. She wished to contribute to my collection and offered me the recipe for Scodelline.

INGREDIENTS:

> *70 g blanched grated almonds*
> *5 tablespoons castor sugar*
> *5 egg yolks*
> *1 egg white*
> *grated lemon rind*

Put the sugar into a saucepan together with 5 tablespoons of water. Bring it to the boil and, stirring constantly, continue to simmer until the sugar begins to thicken. Remove the saucepan from the heat before the sugar darkens.

Add the almonds and continue to stir until the sugar has cooled. Add the egg yolks, blending one egg yolk into the sugar before adding the next.

Put the mixture into a double boiler and, over a low heat, continue to stir until the mixture thickens and the froth disappears from the surface.

Remove from the heat and, continuing to stir, add the lemon rind. Continue to stir until the mixture has cooled completely.

Beat the egg whites until very stiff. Gently fold the beaten egg whites into the mixture. When the mixture is well blended spoon it into individual serving cups and sprinkle the top with cinnamon. Serve chilled and decorated with a candied cherry.

Matzot Cake

For well over a century, the Italian matzots were baked in a Florentine bakery run by a small Jewish congregation and, I believe they are still baked there.

Unlike the new matzot, which are the same as Australian matzots, the old Italian matzot are about half a metre in diameter and about 12 mm thick. The taste of the Italian matzot is similar to our matzots but the Italian matzot is not crisp.

I do not know how the Italian matzot is packaged now, but in the past, Italian matzots were sold packed in wicker baskets.

This recipe, as well as the matzot, is from Tuscany.

INGREDIENTS:

> 5 tablespoons castor sugar
> 1 tablespoon water
> ½ teaspoon cinnamon
> 4 eggs
> 1 thick Italian matzot
> grated rind of 1 lemon

Soak the matzot in water, overnight.

Strain the soaked matzot through a cheese cloth and squeeze dry. Put the matzot into a mixing bowl, and set aside.

Make a syrup with 5 tablespoons of sugar, 1 tablespoon of water and the cinnamon. When the sugar has melted pour it over the soaked matzot.

Separate the eggs and add the egg yolks to the matzot until well amalgamated.

Beat the egg whites until stiff. Fold the beaten egg white into the matzot mixture. Spoon the mixture into a round oiled baking tin and bake in a preheated oven, at 350°F or 180°C, for about 45 minutes.

When the cake is cold dust with icing sugar.

Matzot Meal Frittelle

INGREDIENTS:

> *4 tablespoons castor sugar*
> *4 tablespoons fine matzot meal*
> *2 tablespoons sultanas*
> *2 tablespoons pine nuts*
> *4 eggs*
> *olive oil for frying*

Separate the eggs and whisk the egg yolks with the sugar until very light and frothy. Add the other ingredients and mix until well amalgamated.

Beat the egg whites until stiff then gently fold the beaten egg whites into the mixture.

Heat the oil in a frying pan and when the oil is very hot drop the mixture into the oil one tablespoon at a time. When the frittelle are golden brown turn and fry until they are well coloured on both sides. Remove the frittelle from the oil and arrange them on several sheets of paper towels.

Keep the frittelle on the paper towels, in a warm oven, until ready to serve. Before serving them, dust the frittelle with castor sugar or cover with liquefied honey.

Index